P

C000184573

THE GREAT
STEAM
CHASE

The Last Days of Steam on BR's SOUTHERN REGION

KEITH WIDDOWSON

The History Press

To my wife Joan and daughter Victoria for their
tolerance with an obsessive hobby and the many
hours spent entombed in the garden shed or
'office' during its compilation.

First published 2013

The History Press
The Mill, Brimscombe Port
Stroud, Gloucestershire, GL5 2QG
www.thehistorypress.co.uk

British Library Cataloguing in Publication Data.
A catalogue record for this book is available from the British Library.

ISBN 978 0 7524 7957 6

Typesetting and origination by The History Press
Printed in Great Britain

CONTENTS

INTRODUCTION

I t was while I was on the morning dog walk, sheltering from the rain in a hay barn at a farm in Somerset during the summer of August 2009, that I made the decision to write a further tome of my chasing of the 'Iron Horse'. Iron horse is a description often used when referring to steam locomotives. Originally the earliest railways consisted of carriages being drawn along rails by horses. When the steam engine was introduced the horses were 'retired' and because it was doing the work previously performed by horses, the association stuck. The term is believed to have originated in the 1840s when the encroachment across America by the railroad companies into native Indian territories was in its heyday.

My first book – about my European travels – had yet to hit the market but, having had several articles accepted and published within the railway-orientated monthlies, I took solace in the fact that there was an interest in what I had to say! To pass the time while waiting for the rain to stop (the Met Office had unwisely declared 2009 to be a barbecue summer earlier in the year – a major misjudgement on par with the hurricane denial of 1987) I began jotting down on scraps of paper my first thoughts – prior to visiting the nearby East Somerset Railway later that day. We were staying near Radstock, a town long devoid of railways, at a farm adjacent to the Frome to Bristol branch line which had closed to passengers in 1959. Walking the route (it had been converted to a Sustrans cycleway) with my dog the 1½ miles to the nearest pub at Kilmersdon, I'd visualise the scene passengers might have witnessed over half a century earlier. The line, built by entrepreneurial speculators hoping for big profits, never paid its way and the sparse service on offer, provided by the inevitable GWR tank locomotive and two coaches, was invariably condemned to closure – even pre-Beeching. Back to 2009 and that year, resulting from the economic recession and enticed by the promise of a good summer here in Britain, many people had diverted from their usual European beach holiday in search of a cheaper alternative at home. Other factors such as air traffic control strikes increased security checks because of terrorist attacks and swine 'flu perhaps also came into the equation – little did we know volcanic ash was just around the corner! So that's it, the decision was made – but while the subject was obviously going to be about my railway travels, what title and region would I select? My first tome, entitled *The Great Iron Horse Chase: Europe*, was (fingers crossed) in the hope that it would be the first in a series, with others following with a geographic variation – eventually perhaps covering all the areas of Britain I had visited during the mid-1960s. I had chased the Iron Horse all over the UK until its extinction in August of 1968 and with the most prolific area covered being southern Britain, I came to the conclusion that a tome highlighting these exploits would be most appropriate. Allhallows-on-Sea to Exmouth and Padstow to Ilfracombe was the length of coastline over which the Southern Region (née Railway) held almost undisputed sway and to which Sunny South Sam (a 1930s advertising poster personality) exhorted the public to go for sunshine trips to the coast. Regional boundary changes during 1963 had reallocated the railway system west of Salisbury to the Western Region but I am confident, enacting the writer's license, the reader will have no objection if I include my visits to Devon and Cornwall here. Will you join me on my journeys during those far off halcyon days of the steam locomotive travel?

The final steam locomotive to be constructed was Class 9F 2–10–0 No. 92220 at Swindon. The naming of the locomotive, *Evening Star,* was by British Transport Commission member Mr R.F. Hanks on 18 March 1960 who said:

> There had to be a last steam locomotive and it is a tremendous thing that it should be built here in these great works at Swindon. I am sure it has been truly said that no other product of man's mind has ever exercised such a compelling hold upon the public's imagination as the steam locomotive. No other machine in its day has been a more faithful friend to mankind nor has contributed more to the growth of industry in this, the land of its birth and indeed throughout the whole world . . . those who have lived in the steam age of railways will carry the most nostalgic memories right to the end.

How right he was! What do I remember about steam trains before I joined BR? The answer I'm afraid is not a lot. With a travelsick dog and two sons, my parents made most trips by car (a very large Humber bought from a neighbour for £10 and which my Dad once positioned over a tree stump in a field when parking for a picnic, breaking the rear axle). During the summer holidays I vaguely recall Mum (Dad was at work) taking us on a day trip to the coast and, having travelled by EMU from home (St Mary Cray) to Sevenoaks, catching a main line train at the head of which was what I subsequently identified as an Unmodified Bulleid Pacific. Another recollection was that of a steam locomotive (later recognised as a Maunsell Mogul) disturbing the tranquillity of our estate while struggling to restart a lengthy freight service up the bank (1 in 132) opposite my house (adjacent to the St Mary Cray to Bickley line) having deposited or collected coal wagons in the siding there. The line there was doubled to a four-track railway during the late 1950s as part of the first phase of the Kent Coast electrification scheme and, amid the Wimpy diggers, tractors and infrastructure debris, while rising for my paper round at about 6 in the morning a steam train, seemingly calling at St Mary Cray, was often espied, and heard whistling on its way coast-bound – the diet of mundane EMUs being the norm.

The longest and regrettably never documented trips were with Dad when we went visiting our relations at Leicester. He made them twice a year – my younger brother going with him on the summer trip while I suffered the cold, often late and weather-delayed winter trip. Loaded with Christmas presents on a Sunday every December we caught an EMU to Elephant & Castle, Northern Line to King's Cross and then along the Midland line to Leicester (London Road). What locos were at the front – Scots, Jubilees, etc. – and they were never noted! Apparently until the rationalisation of services on the ex-Great Central we used to travel by the day excursion ticket out of Marylebone to Leicester Central – it being better positioned for our three location visits within the city. What did I travel with then I wonder –

A3s perhaps, or maybe, V2s? I once asked Dad to detail the dates so that I might get a letter published in an attempt to identify any haulages, but he was unsure of them and so it would have been like looking for a needle in a haystack. Engineering work and fog often delayed our return journey and I remember on one occasion we were so late that we had to catch one of the hourly early morning services down the Catford Loop specifically provided in those days to get print workers home. I was still sent to school later that morning! By my commencement of BR employment, Kent was virtually steamless and, as described in the opening chapter, the addictive draw of the steam locomotive didn't materialise until the daily sight and sound of them at Waterloo.

1

WATERLOO: WHERE IT ALL STARTED

May I be allowed, firstly, to set the scene as to when and where the seeds of my love of the Iron Horse were initially sown? The first 3½ years of my career with British Rail, which commenced in June 1962, were based at the impressive General Manager's Offices at Waterloo. From my office, perched high up on the fourth floor, panoramic views of London were available if looking north, while there was just a massive expanse of glass-covered roof if looking south. In the summer you could sunbathe on the flat-roofed top of the offices, next to the beehives, adjacent to which were the massive water tanks which supplied the entire station's requirements, but with no railings and long drops all around, great care was needed. Although above the roof you could still hear all the station announcements and general noise emanating from the activities below – the major ones were the arrivals (platforms 12–14) and departures (platforms 9–11) of the steam-operated services.

Not initially an enthusiast when joining British Railways, it was not until mid-1963 that any interest in disappearing steam and line closures finally fired sufficient interest to propel me out to places I had often directed telephone callers to as my job as telephone enquiry clerk. As a gopher (errand boy/office junior) I was sent all over Waterloo station – often having to descend into the labyrinth of archways and offices secreted in its bowels. For beneath Waterloo's concourse, away from the passages used by thousands of commuters hurrying along to either the Bakerloo/ Northern lines or the 'Drain' to Bank, there were a myriad of establishments accessed through warm, distillery-smelling passageways. One such underground thoroughfare was known as the 'Long Valley' – the main usage of which was for the then extensive parcels traffic – off which there were side tunnels to the staff canteen, police offices and catering depots. At street level there was Lower Road with its range of arches containing parcel offices, lost property (staff could have their pick on Wednesdays 12.00 to 13.00 hours) and commercial offices where the region's line closure notices were dispatched from – one of each issue unfailingly always falling into my hands! If you knew where to look an amateur dramatic society was located in an archway (opposite the appropriately named Hole in the Wall pub) in Meopham Street. There were also commercial warehouses some of which contained alcohol from which the aforementioned smell came. During the Second World War a bomb set light thousands of gallons of bonded spirits, which burned so fiercely that the station was closed to all traffic for a week until the

PRICE ONE SHILLING

Passenger

Services

Timetable

LONDON
Victoria
Waterloo
Charing Cross
London Bridge
Cannon Street
Holborn Viaduct
and the
SOUTH-EAST
SOUTH & WEST
OF ENGLAND

MAIN LINE
AND SUBURBAN

17th JUNE to 8th SEPTEMBER 1963

SOUTHERN
BRITISH RAILWAYS

Left: The front cover of the telephone enquiry clerks' well thumbed 'bible' from which we directed customers on their journeys throughout the Southern Region.

BR 6629/19

BRITISH RAILWAYS

SOUTHERN REGION

STAFF

ASSOCIATION

MEMBER'S CARD

Right: The necessary membership card required to gain access to cheap beer and food – the club being at the centre of many social activities with fellow railwaymen.

brickwork supporting the track above had cooled down and was strengthened with temporary girders.

Off of the passage leading from the concourse to Waterloo Road was the BRSA (British Railways Staff Association) club. For a pittance a week deducted from your wages you could become a member there, in turn qualifying for entry to all the many BRSA establishments located at each major depot throughout the region, at which you could quaff cheap beer and food and enjoy a game of darts with fellow railwaymen. This location was the scene of my many sporting triumphs (darts, pool and crib), the trophies of which, much to my wife's annoyance, still reside at home, albeit collecting dust. We were all part of a great big family and, because my friends and colleagues came from all over the region, it became the hub of our social life for many years.

A frequent collecting place for London's homeless population was Leake Street (a road running underneath the width of Waterloo station connecting York Way to the market in Lower Marsh) where they were attracted by the warm, cosy, dry environment – at midnight, the Salvation Army soup van making a regular visit. At the other end of the spectrum I was often sent to the plush carpeted top bosses' offices on the second floor, never actually seeing them but having to deal with their secretaries. Occasionally a visit to the station announcer's 'crows nest' was required of me from which a wonderful view of the entire station (from just under the roof) was obtained.

Ardent postage stamp collecting managers often dispatched me to the post office where many hours were spent queuing for first day covers. In later years commercial organisations had stands on the concourse where they gave away

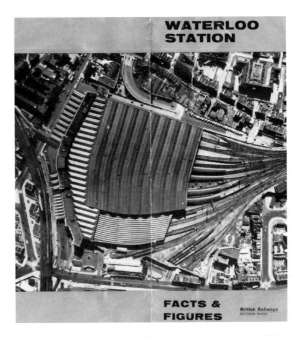

WATERLOO STATION

FACTS & FIGURES

British Railways SOUTHERN REGION

The SR publicity department's pamphlet detailing the facts and figures about Waterloo station.

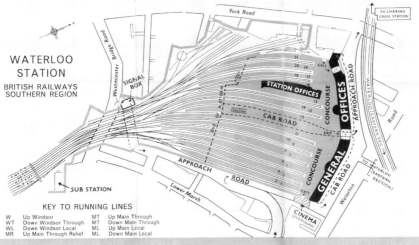

WATERLOO STATION

BRITISH RAILWAYS SOUTHERN REGION

KEY TO RUNNING LINES

W	Up Windsor	MT	Up Main Through
WT	Down Windsor Through	MT	Down Main Through
WL	Down Windsor Local	ML	Up Main Local
MR	Up Main Through Relief	ML	Down Main Local

Waterloo is the busiest station on the Southern Region of British Railways.

Every normal weekday, it handles 1,238 trains and 194,063 passengers. In a year it deals with nearly 600,000 seat reservations.

It occupies 24½ acres and has 31 running roads 21 platforms with a total platform length of 14,626 ft. The longest, No. 11, is 946 ft.

At peak times the station is working to full capacity— and the number of passengers continues to grow. In 1939 the daily figure was 156,497. Since then the number in the heaviest single hour of the peak has almost doubled —from 25,929 to 46,697

From Waterloo there are direct express trains to the West Country, to Bournemouth and to the docks at Southampton and Weymouth, fast electric trains to Portsmouth (for the Isle of Wight ferries), and suburban electric trains to most parts of Surrey, South Middlesex and into Hampshire. Three best known long distance trains are the Bournemouth Belle, Royal Wessex and Atlantic Coast Express.

The heaviest train is the 1 10 a.m. newspaper train to the West Country. Its loaded weight is about 450 tons, it serves 95 stations and covers 479 miles.

Many trains call at Clapham Junction to connect with services from Victoria.

One busy summer Saturday, 119 main line trains left the station carrying 45,386 holidaymakers.

The power-operated signal box, built in 1936, has 309 miniature levers, 12 train describers and 148 track circuits.

The original Waterloo Station was opened in 1848 and the present station in 1922.

There is access from the station to the Southern's Waterloo & City line, which has Britain's first Travolator —a 312 ft. long moving pavement—at the Bank end, and to the LTE Underground station, also to the Waterloo (Eastern) station, etc.

free samples of their newest chocolate bars, cereals, crisps, etc. I was sent time and time again to collect the 'freebies' for many staff members too lazy to queue themselves. There were many unique sights often observed on my errand-running. The SR Railway Orphanage at Woking always had a dog (an Airedale?) and owner prowling the concourse with a collecting box on its back. Then there were the shoeshine boys, the extraordinary hats the ladies wore on their way to Ascot, the large groups of West Indian families awaiting their relations from the Southampton Dock trains planning to start a new life here, the TV personalities passing through and finally those nervously waiting under the station clock on an obvious blind date.

The most famous of all departures was of course Winston Churchill's funeral train. Although operationally the Oxfordshire-bound train would have suited the authorities better if it had been from Paddington, Churchill was adamant that it should be from Waterloo – allegedly saying 'If De Gaulle dies before I do, I don't give a damn where the train leaves from. Otherwise, it has to go from Waterloo.'

The office in which I worked also dealt with all the bookings and reservations of Camping Coaches throughout the Southern Region, and very popular they were too – the only condition of occupancy being that you had to travel by train to/from your holiday. We made sure they did – we sold them the tickets! The complete list of locations escapes me but I do remember that some were positioned at the New Forest stations of Lyndhurst Road, Hinton Admiral and Sway. The vehicles themselves were redundant Pullman vehicles, gutted and made into living accommodation big enough to hold large families, and while the resident station staff could deal with all on site problems and requirements the initial booking was at Waterloo. I well remember the busiest times were always January to March each year when everyone wanted to book the same school weeks or public holiday weeks for the summer (nothing's changed then!). We had a large board on the wall with the person's name on the required week and location on a yellow ticket – changed to blue upon receipt of their money. In November of 1964 a static exhibition using one of the coaches was held at Waterloo and Victoria stations and I was proud to be selected as an assistant on board (I was only seventeen), my duties being to distribute pamphlets and answer any questions the public asked. By then the increasing addiction to steam haulage was manifesting within me and aware that, at Waterloo, the coach had to be shunted from the North Carriage Sidings to the main platforms (via West Crossings) sometime after the morning rush hour, I volunteered to travel on the shunt using the excuse that windows need to be opened and kettle switched on, etc. This proved a smart move because of the three days the exhibition was on, the motive power was Standard Tank Nos 82013, 82023 and West Country 34103 Calstock – the latter two drivers giving me a footplate ride. Needless to say the Victoria shunt from Grosvenor sidings to the main station was with less interesting electric or diesel locomotives.

During my lunch break the 13.30 departure for Weymouth and Bournemouth West was often viewed from the end of platform 11 and perhaps it was the sheer majesty of the Bulleid Pacific with its safety valves lifting and the fireman fuelling the fire in readiness for the 143-mile journey ahead, that sowed the seeds for a lifetime hobby. As I stood there, camera poised in readiness for the platform staff's whistle and the guard's 'right away', the potent power subsequently unleashed as the Pacific initially slipped (an inherent Bulleid weakness) on the greasy rail before finally finding her feet and powering the train into the distance must have sunk

A regular departure often viewed during my lunch break at Waterloo was the lightweight (three-coach) 13.54 stopping service for Basingstoke. Pictured under 'that cavernous roof', 'West Country' Pacific No. 34031 *Torrington* (withdrawn three months later) prepares herself for departure on 27 October 1964.

Was this departure, regularly witnessed from Waterloo's longest platform (11), the catalyst that sowed the seeds for a lifetime hobby? One of the magnificent 'Merchant Navy's, No. 35021 *New Zealand Line,* readies herself with the 13.30 Weymouth departure on 29 April 1964. She was withdrawn in August 1965 – before I had the opportunity for a run with her.

Paraphrasing Otis Redding's hit of the 1960s, sittin' on the dock of the bay is one of Nine Elms' stud of BR 3MTs, No. 82023. Displaced from various parts of the country, in this case Devon, these tanks were to monopolise the ECS workings here at Waterloo and Clapham Yard during the final years. This shot was taken on 28 January 1966.

deep into the memory bank of an impressionable teenager. At the rear of the train, ably assisting with an almighty push was the tank engine, which had brought the stock in from Clapham Yard. Within the cavernous station train shed the ear-splitting cacophony of its thunderous exhaust sent the pigeons into orbit and made any conversation nigh on impossible. It all lasted for less than a minute before the tank engine driver slammed on the brakes to bring him to a stand alongside the ever-present gaggle of trainspotters always resident at the country end of platform 11. How anyone can fail to be impressed with the sight and sound of a steam locomotive in full flight is STILL is beyond my comprehension.

Infrequently visiting Waterloo these days I can still, among the hum of electrics and throb of diesels, recollect so vividly the aforementioned scenario. Had I of course been present an hour earlier I would have witnessed the 12.30 departure of the prestige all Pullman 'Bournemouth Belle'. This lighter loaded service did not require any additional propulsion upon its exit from Waterloo – perhaps being just as well as the first course of soup could well have been served! You could just observe the clientele, partially hidden by the window curtains, settling back into the

Eastleigh-allocated BR Standard 4MT No. 76012 is seen here at Waterloo on 28 January 1966 with the 15.38 Parcels service for her home station. She wasn't to survive the year – being withdrawn that September.

Awaiting the road on 16 February 1965 from Waterloo's platform 11 for Nine Elms is BR 5MT No. 73114 *Etarre*. Twenty of this class, when allocated new to the SR in the late 1950s, were named (much to the chagrin of SR devotees) after the 'King Arthur' locomotives they displaced. Photographers wishing panoramic shots of steam services on the approaches at Waterloo often visited the flats in the distance – much to the annoyance of residents.

plush seats facing their cloth-covered, lamp-adorned tables. What different worlds did they inhabit – would a lowly clerk such as myself one day be able to afford to travel in such luxury? With a greater amount of action on offer I sometimes travelled to Clapham Junction to view not just the Waterloo expresses but any yard activities and Inter-Regional freights – always noting that many platform ends had 'resident' spotters equipped with chairs, food and notepads having settled in for a long stay. For the best photographs of departing trains from Waterloo, a block of high-rise flats (Canterbury Rise?) near St Thomas' Hospital became a regular visiting point. Towards the end of steam, however, the occupants became somewhat vociferous at the increasing numbers of us 'camping out' (being the days before secure/number only entry) with photographic positions having to be relocated up or down a level depending on the ferocity of the complaints!

The railways, certainly prior to the issue of *The Reshaping of British Railways* published in 1963, seemed to be stuck in a time warp. Everything went on as it always had done but both Dr Beeching's plans for wholesale closures and modernisation was on the horizon. Taking the report first, it proposed (the government always had the final say) that 18,000 miles of railways, 6,000 of which were mostly rural branch and cross-country routes, should close – together with 2,363 (in reality over 3,000) stations nationally, which were to have their services

Taken from 'those flats' is Nine Elms' 'West Country' No. 34021 *Dartmoor* approaching Waterloo with the 10.08 ex-Bournemouth West on 20 May 1965. The Lower Marsh's market cafés, seen in the background, were much frequented by myself over the years – never getting to my Kent home until late each day due to commuting on steam services into Surrey or Hampshire each evening.

Taken from the spotters' end of platform 11 at Waterloo, BR Standard 4MT No. 80143 storms away from the station with a single van during February 1965.

withdrawn in an attempt to make the railways financially self-sufficient. Coupled with the announcement the following year of the Bournemouth line electrification, the inevitable conclusion – i.e. that of the demise of steam traction on the SR – was palpable. The electrification plan stated that while the electrification between Pirbright Junction (Brookwood) and Branksome was financially viable, the remaining 32 miles to Weymouth was not and that nineteen Type 3 (later designated Class 33) diesel locomotives were to be converted to push-pull mode for services over that section. The seemingly 'insufficient funds for complete electrification were 'found' some twenty-one years later, thus highlighting the short-sightedness associated with money for any and every railway modernisation project – no change there then! In the immediate surroundings in SE1, changes were also happening with many photographs of steam at Waterloo station having the backdrop of the then futuristic Shell building – a concrete monstrosity still standing nowadays albeit a little weather-stained and having been converted into private accommodation. The Windsor line platforms, having been dramatically altered and thus changing the original neat overall appearance of the station to accommodate the lengthy Eurostar services, are now lying dormant waiting appropriate funding to return them to domestic use again.

The 14.10 empty Milks departure from Waterloo for Clapham Yard (en route to the West Country), rostered for a BR 3MT, had super power on 28 January 1966 in the form of BR 5MT No. 73170.

An unidentified BR 3MT wanders into Waterloo station during February 1965 with the Milk empties from Vauxhall. The 1936-built signal-box was demolished in the early 1990s to make way for the short-lived Eurostar terminal.

Lunchtime visits to Clapham Junction often resulted in viewing representatives of classes not so frequently seen at Waterloo – ex-SR No. 31811 being an example. She was photographed on 1 October 1964 awaiting signals in the Up fast loop – this Guildford-allocated locomotive being withdrawn in August of the following year.

Another example of the benefits of a Clapham Junction lunchtime visit was to observe the transfer freights from the WR/LMR to Norwood. Here Rugby's ex-LMS 8F No. 48122 restarts from a signal stop on 1 October 1964 – she was to end her days at the Welsh shed of Croes Newydd in February 1967.

Some years later I purchased a copy of the British Transport film *Terminus*. Filmed in 1962 it depicts twenty-four hours in the life of Waterloo station and it is wonderfully accurate in its portrayal of every facet of life at a big London terminus and is exactly as I remember it – a happy workplace and workforce fondly remembered. The intention of 'setting the scene' of my early forays into Iron Horse chasing has hopefully thus been achieved.

2

AN ADDICTION
EXPLAINED

During the final eighteen months [to Jul 67] ever more men and youths had turned over their spare time to the pursuit of steam. It was essentially a masculine activity, the appearance of a young (or not so young) lady being extremely rare. Psychologists would probably view the activity as an extension of primitive hunting instincts, a desire to be in at the kill. As far as we know there have been no historical or sociological studies of the behaviour of railway enthusiasts during the final years of Southern steam, but there is plenty of evidence of the level of commitment practiced by its devotees.

The above extract (source unknown) describes exactly the 'symptoms' associated with the near-frenzied scenario witnessed and participated in by myself. Having initially joined BR because my parents noted my interest in local timetables (albeit bus), I soon realised that the majority, certainly, of the clerical workforce not only saw their employment as a means to pay the mortgage but as an extension of their hobby – enhanced perhaps by the free and reduced rate travel facilities available! One particular friend, Bill – with whom I was to subsequently travel throughout Europe, often arrived in the office on a Monday morning with tales of his travels, photographs and timetables from all over the country. 'Get out there – use your travel facilities. It's all disappearing,' he often said. He was referring to the seemingly relentless number of routes closing as a result of Dr Beeching's axe together with the associated increasing dieselisation – the combination of which resulted in the wholesale slaughter of the Iron Horse.

During the latter part of 1963 curiosity began to get the better of me and I tentatively started to venture further afield, away from the comfortable suburban journeys undertaken so far, to routes threatened with closure. During those early explorations I regrettably failed to document any details and it was only by carrying a Brownie 127 camera and an ever-deteriorating flimsy paper network map on which I coloured the relevant routes, that any proof of journeys made survived the years. From the March of 1964, however, having had a birthday present from my parents of a Kodak Colorsnap 35 and now always travelling with a notebook, the addiction was taking hold of me. Line closures were continuing at an unbelievable pace throughout the early to mid-1960s in what turned out to be an abortive attempt to make BR pay its way. These actions only served to make prospective travellers realise that having had to use cars to start and end their journeys, they may as well use them throughout – BR being the loser again. Most of the lines affected had been neglected by BR (i.e. infrastructure/dieselisation) and therefore often retained steam power. Upon the realisation that the 1955 BR modernisation plan, envisaging the elimination of steam traction by 1968, meant that my hobby was heading for oblivion, my interests began to swing from that of a line basher into the chasing of the Iron Horse itself. There was little time left!

As the months counted down an ever-increasing number of enthusiasts could be witnessed on the scene. Some decided a photographic record was for them and could be seen at the lineside whenever another 'last' occasion was occurring. Others, myself included, decided to obtain runs behind as many different steam locomotives as possible. We, the haulage bashers, always considered ourselves a cut above the rest. It was easy enough to 'spot' or photograph an engine whether it was on the scrap line, working a freight or van service or at rest in a depot but, for us to redline our entry in our copies of the *Locoshed Book* it had to be in action *and* working a passenger train. The resulting satisfaction of seeing a page or column completed, perhaps even before our fellow conspirators, was without doubt what we all wanted to achieve. It was a challenge, the thrill of the chase, which spurred us on.

Photography was always, as far as I was concerned, secondary to the pursuit of steam haulage – I would have loved to have been at the lineside as well but being unable to be in both places at once, a choice had to be made. It was a race against time. Success in tracking down steam-operated services came with experience but it was always reassuring to see a wisp of smoke in the distance thus increasing the likelihood, but not always guaranteeing, the arrival of one. Many of us purchased season tickets from London to Southampton and could be seen most evenings on rush

The necessary paraphernalia required to accompany me on my travels over the years.

hour services from Waterloo hunting out all the locomotives, homing in on the 'speed merchants' (drivers who willingly thrashed their machines to achieve high speeds). It was a mad, frenetic period – the camaraderie, the sense of urgency – knowing it would all end one day. I sometimes wonder whether such activities would ever have occurred if had the steam engine not been dying so quickly. While appreciating the run-down condition and constant failures, such a frequent occurrence towards the end, I still feel privileged to have had witnessed the scenario and participated in the chases with all its attendant emotional excitement and sadness.

Musically it was a great period to live through. There was *Top of the Pops* – or I could listen illegally to Radio Luxembourg under the bedclothes on my Pye transistor radio – with the Beatles and Rolling Stones dominating the charts. Then there was the Kinks capturing the sense of occasion with their hit 'Waterloo Sunset' based on the cessation of steam at Waterloo (or was that purely coincidental?) and even the national media (including those pirate radio stations moored outside British waters) credited some air space to the event. My small attaché case (16in x 10in x 4in) accompanied me on all of my travels. All necessary requirements were contained within it – timetables, camera, Ian Allan books, notebook, Lyons pies, Club biscuits, pens, flannel, handkerchief, stopwatch, cartons of orange drinks, sandwiches and of course a BR1 carriage key – a necessary piece of equipment to obtain a few hours' sleep in vehicles stabled in the carriage sidings! Sturdy enough to sit on in crowded corridors of packed trains and doubling up as a pillow (albeit hard!) on overnight services, the case was in regular use through the final years of BR steam and even travelled with me throughout Europe in 1968/9. Having survived many domestic upheavals over the years it now enjoys a comfortable retirement at the bottom of my 'railway' cupboard at home – containing all the documented travel information without which I could never have contemplated writing a book such as this. As for dress apparel the anorak was not in existence then – to the best of my knowledge it was a duffel coat with toggle fasteners. Usually having come from a day's work at the office the obligatory tie (modern and straight-edged) was always worn – albeit at peculiar angles after an overnight trip. The followers were classless. They came from all walks of life including vicars, MPs (Robert Adley of Winchester, for example, who became a leading opponent to privatisation) and persons from many varied occupations. I often wondered how those who did not obtain cheap travel as an employment perk could afford it all – but then again ticket checks on trains were infrequent and there were no automatic barriers back then!

Upon returning home after each escapade (or within a few days if very late back) all the necessary details collected were transferred into legibility within large A4 sized desk diaries. Separate small books kept individual locomotive mileages, shed visits and timed trains. I lost the pre-June 1965 notebooks from which I extracted the information but have retained all the rest. There was much to do. Each 'capture' was redlined in the Ian Allan *Locoshed Book* – if the loco entry was blacked-out then it had been withdrawn! These books were reissued quite regularly and what with the continuous transferring (information courtesy of *Railway World* magazine) around of locomotives resulting from line and depot closures, much midnight oil was burned in just attempting to keep it all up to date. This of course became a nationwide hobby so it wasn't just the 200 or so Southern Region-based locomotives. Luckily the detailing of such minutiae came easy to me through my work as a BR train planner where precise and accurate documentation was a necessary requirement.

3

THE JOURNEY BEGINS

My original intention – that of taking the reader on a geographical journey the length of the Southern Region of British Railways from Kent to Cornwall – was vetoed by my daughter because, having often revisited steam-infested areas on several occasions over the years, she highlighted that it could lead to a disparate collection of unlinked stories perhaps not easily flowing together – her suggestion that I relate my travels chronologically being subsequently adopted. From March 1964 *every* non-commuting railway journey I made was methodically documented commencing with that trip as number 1 and finishing with the final number 425 in July 1967, which, if detailed here, would probably cause the reader an apoplexy. Not all, however, were SR-based, as I increasingly had to travel throughout Britain in search of steam. Some jaunts were just evening visits to Woking while others were 5 nights and 6 days up north. Prior to that March, and only with aforementioned faded prints from my Brownie 127 bearing witness to my visits, I travelled over branch lines threatened with closure such as Guildford to Horsham, New Romney and Hayling Island – the latter, luckily caught just a week from closure. Researching this book led me to realise that the only SR line closure I missed after that first visit to a 'doomed' line in November 1963, was the Romsey to Andover branch which closed in September 1964. I can only attribute this miss because it was worked by DEMUs and, by that date, I was already concentrating on steam services. The Hayling Island branch line, the junction of which was at Havant, modernised like most of the stations involved in the 1930s 'Electric Coast' scheme by the Southern Railway, remained steam-operated until its demise. Although the carriages were relatively 'modern' it was the motive power that was Victorian. The 1,100ft-long weight-restricted timber bridge across Langstone Harbour and sharp curves en route resulted in the only class of locomotive permitted to cross it being Stroudley's diminutive 0–6–0T A1Xs – known affectionately as 'Terriers' on account of their distinctive 'bark' of the exhaust beat. The disparity in size of the tall-chimneyed tanks (which had monopolised the services for over sixty years) and their stock belied their ability to take the train on its 4½-mile journey – the evocative scenario being helped by the Westinghouse brake pump wheezing and thumping its syncopated rhythm. The service, referred to locally as 'The Hayling Billy', in the summer saw vast numbers of holidaymakers requiring an intensive four trains per hour four-carriage service just to cope. The line's future, however, was decided, as always, by infrastructure costs – the speed-restricted (20 mph) timber swing bridge over Langstone Harbour was in a serious state of neglect. With the annual operating profit of a mere £2,000 per annum and the bridge requiring £40,000 expenditure, the inevitable closure came

My first 'closure' visit. On 26 October 1963 the subsequently preserved ex-LBSCR AIX 0–6–0T No. 32650 waits at Havant with a Hayling Island service. The line was closed a week later, infrastructure costs associated with the poor condition of the bridge over Langstone Harbour being cited as the reason.

A visit to Ashford Works (on the pretext of route learning having recently obtained promotion to DMO SED Queen Street), ex-SECR 0–6–0 DS239 (formerly No. 31592) was caught on 31 March 1966. Withdrawal the following year led to eventual preservation at the Bluebell Railway.

in November 1963. Luckily for present-day enthusiasts several of these unique locomotives have been restored and can be seen at work on a number of preserved railways in southern England.

Another class of tank locomotive that, similar to the A1Xs, became extinct during 1963 was Wainwright's 0–4–4T H class. These were to be found eking their days out working push-pull trains – two of which, if memory serves me correctly, I travelled with on an early afternoon Three Bridges to Tunbridge Wells train. Vaguely recalling the train being double-headed as far as East Grinstead – by leaning out of the window approaching Tunbridge Wells I managed to photograph sister 31544 at the motive power depot – nowadays the station at Tunbridge Wells is in use as the HQ of the Spa Valley Railway. Three Bridges has subsequently been completely engulfed within the inexorable urban expansion of the Crawley and Gatwick area and I am certain that present-day commuters from East Grinstead would have benefitted had the 6¾-mile connecting branch not been closed in 1967. The nearby then embryonic Bluebell Railway was visited in September 1963 just prior to the electrified main line connection, between Haywards Heath and Ardingly, being closed.

The confidence was growing and I began to travel further afield from my Kent home. They felt like expeditions into the unknown – oblivious to any dangers and enjoying the freedom and spirit of adventure often allied to youth. It also broadened my geographic knowledge of the land of my birth and helped considerably when dealing with customers when working at the CTEB at Waterloo.

With the Beatles songs swamping the American charts and the launch of England's first pirate radio ship, *Caroline*, it was in March 1964 that my first *documented* journey with steam was made. The Kent coast electrification schemes of 1959 (North) and 1962 (South) had effectively rendered the steam locomotive almost, but not quite, extinct in Kent. Excluding several ancient works pilots at Ashford (photographed during a 'route knowledge appreciation' visit in March 1966, having recently changed jobs) the only remaining location in the county to witness steam was at Tonbridge from where some services from Redhill to Tunbridge Wells and Eastbourne were still steam operated. I was with my local YHA group and an overnight visit to the Blackboys hostel (between Crowborough and Rotherfield) was the reason for the trip. Waiting at Tonbridge as a connection off of our nondescript electric train was one of the BR-designed tank engines which were built during the 1950s as a replacement for more elderly worn-out types inherited upon nationalisation in 1947. Standard Tank No. 80140 of Redhill shed, an engine I was to chance across several years later while working the 'Kenny Belle', took us the few miles en route to Crowborough from where we 'yomped' through the Sussex countryside to the hostel, arriving just before nightfall. Cooking our own food, making our own beds, sleeping in a dormitory of a dozen or so snoring friends – it was all a revelation to a young lad who had only known the comfort of home. Little was I to know that, over the next five years I was to spend hundreds of nights roughing it on trains and platforms in my pursuit of steam!

Anyway, back to that trip. After breakfast had been enjoyed, and the associated 'leave the accommodation as you found it' scenario was effected, we trudged wearily through the pouring rain and cold wind, arriving at Rotherfield where I

An example of the form necessary to be completed by every BR employee on each occasion a journey was made in order to achieve a 75 per cent reduction on a public fare.

BRITISH RAILWAYS/LONDON TRANSPORT			Request Form for Privilege Ticket/s (Not Transferable). B.R.6599/11	

Name and Initials of Employee (Active or Retired) or Widow M_____(Block letters)

	Male	Female	CLASS (in words)	SINGLE OR RETURN
SELF				
WIFE*		/	FROM	
CHILDREN:— 3 and under 15 years of age (subject to income limit)			TO	
15 years of age and under 21 (subject to income limit)			No/s of Ticket/s Issued	Initials of Booking Clerk.
21 years of age or over (wholly dependent)				

*Cross out when issued under authority to dependent female relative acting as housekeeper and insert "HOUSEKEEPER".
I hereby apply for ticket/s as above (subject to the Regulations and Conditions printed on the Application Form for Privilege Ticket Identity Cards) and declare that it is/they are for the use of the person/s above mentioned.

Signed_____ Grade_____

Department_____

Employed at_____ Region_____

IDENTITY CARD/S _____
LETTERS _____
AND _____
NUMBERS _____

IMPORTANT—THIS FORM MUST BE COMPLETED IN INK

Having just 'suffered' an unexpected run with a Crompton diesel the welcome sight of Redhill-allocated BR Standard 4MT No. 80152 rolling into Hellingly with the 09.45 Reading (Southern) to Eastbourne on 27 May 1964 was much appreciated. Did anyone ever endure the 5-hour all stations through-journey of 91¼ miles (18¼mph!).

The grandiose station of Bexhill West, at one time having 4 platforms, is seen on 27 May 1964 with 2H DEMU 1121 forming the 18.45 departure for Crowhurst. The line closed three weeks later.

attempted to complete the Privilege Ticket Form (necessary in those days for all BR employees to qualify for a 75 per cent fare reduction) much to the amusement of other members of the group. Why were they laughing – well my frozen wet hands failed me, and with the train's arrival imminent, the booking clerk (yes stations were still manned on a Sunday in those days) kindly completed it for me, enabling me to continue my journey home – the others losing their smiles when becoming aware of the financial savings I had made!

I returned to the area a few weeks later – this time on a Sussex-wide track bashing trip – and, not being sufficiently knowledgeable as to which trains were steam and which were diesel, was highly annoyed, to say the least, at passing several steam engines while aboard numerous diesel units! With the increasing knowledge gained from observations together with the acquisition of a copy of the relevant steam locomotive duties, I began to home in on train services operated by them. On this particular May day, having travelled on the 09.47 train from Tunbridge Wells to East Grinstead, with Brighton allocated Standard Tank No. 80018, I then went north to Oxted before heading south through Eridge down to Eastbourne, changing en route at Heathfield to catch the 13.40 starting service – a relatively rare catch of

When passing through Tonbridge en route home on 27 May 1964 I leant out of the window (you could do that back then!) and took this shot of Standard 4MTs Nos 80152 and 80094 on the 19.45 departure for Reading (Southern). I caught No. 80152 later that year in the Eridge area while No. 80094 evaded me for two years, eventually being ensnared on the Lymington branch.

one of the 'new' Type 3 diesels (latterly Class 33) working it not being appreciated! My next target was the 9-mile branch line out of Seaford and for novelty value I took a wonderfully scenic ride on a double-decker Southdown bus over the South Downs themselves – arriving at the mist-shrouded town in time to catch the 15.47 service to Lewes. The 18-minute trip past the then-thriving port of Newhaven and alongside the Ouse Estuary took me to the junction station of Lewes before then returning eastward for an hour's bouncy ride in a 1930s-built EMU to the Grade II listed ex-LB&SCR station at Bexhill Central – opened in 1846. In an attempt to cream off the lucrative day-tripper market the rival SE&CR had arrived elsewhere in the town at the less conveniently sited Bexhill West as late as 1902, with a 4½-mile branch line from the Charing Cross/Hastings main line station of Crowhurst.

Once again the potential was not realised and by 1964 the well-underused four-platformed terminus, built in hope of enticing visiting excursion traffic, was within months of closure. The 18.27 departure took just one solitary passenger (myself) to Crowhurst connecting into my homeward-bound London service – a successful day from the point of track coverage notwithstanding the 'high' cost of tickets at 14s 9d.

4

THE FIGURE EIGHT ITINERARY

Whenever line closures were announced, much poring over the relevant timetables late into the night was undertaken. Funds were still limited and rather than making several day trips to each individual line it was cheaper to accomplish as much as possible in one hit; by necessity involving overnight travel. Looking back at some of the itineraries I compiled I can, retrospectively, appreciate that the putting together of complex schedules was always going to be my forte. Was it any wonder that the many hours spent studying timetables prior to embarking on usually complicated tours, incorporating either announced line closures or soon to be dieselised steam services, were to channel my abilities into a useful skill which fortunately provided me with long-term career as a train planner? With the loud and brash Rolling Stones launching their debut album it was in the April of 1964 that this hastily compiled tour was thrown together having learned that the secondary routes through Hampshire between Salisbury/Brockenhurst via Wimborne to Broadstone were closing the following month. I found out later that one of the other routes fortuitously covered within this tour, that between Taunton and Yeovil, was to succumb to the Beeching axe that June and of course the much-lamented cross-country Somerset & Dorset line between Bath and Bournemouth eventually ceased operation in the March of 1966. If the reader follows my tour on the accompanying map it can be seen that I effectively travelled in a figure of eight – which, resulting from the aforementioned closures, can *never* be repeated. Having accompanied Bill, a far more seasoned traveller than I, on my first overnight trip to South Wales the previous month, I was to embark for the very first time on my own. It was a daunting prospect but was to prove a precursor for hundreds of similar journeys over the next few years.

The penultimate Saturday to the first closure saw me boarding the West of England 01.15 newspaper train at Waterloo – sleep not being on the cards because I had to alight at Salisbury, its first stop, during the few minutes' station stop allowed to detach the rear vans containing Wiltshire's post and papers. This was my first experience of night travel behind a steam locomotive. Always travelling as close to the front as possible – smoke from the locomotive seemingly pervaded through any and all of the openings of the coaches – the noise, smell and the reflecting glow from the firebox on bridges and cuttings all contributed to the adventure. I was to appreciate over the coming years that the steam locomotive is a living thing and often had to be treated with TLC to coax the best out of her. Unlike the diesels and electrics where a fault often meant termination, the steam locomotive always (well nearly) got you there.

The lights of London and the suburbs were soon left behind and it was only the comforting glow from the many signal-boxes en route reassuring all was well which broke the inky blackness of the countryside. Upon arrival at Salisbury I walked the length of the station to the Down bay at the eastern end, careful to avoid all the offloading activity of the station staff, to board the 03.17 departure for Weymouth. Setting off back through the tunnel I had only just travelled through before swinging south into deepest Hampshire, one of Bournemouth's competent stud of BR Standard 4MTs, No. 76055, was in charge that morning. I well remember this particular journey, the locomotive shuffling along through the now moonlit countryside leaving a trail of white smoke, stopping on a seemingly as-required basis at the intermediate stations such as Fordingbridge, Daggons Road and Verwood, unloading mails and newspapers from the van transferred off of the London train at Salisbury. My manager at the office I worked was, needless to say, also an enthusiast and used to say (tongue in cheek?) that you couldn't count as having covered a line unless it was during daylight hours and you were awake! I was subsequently able to inform him that the countryside WAS swathed in moonlight and I WAS awake! After a long stop at Broadstone where a large amount of mushroom traffic was dealt with, we took the rarely used northerly line around Holes Bay (a tidal lake to the north of Poole harbour) before continuing the 58-mile journey through Thomas Hardy's 'Wessex Heartland' of the Frome Valley, eventually descending down into the seaside resort of Weymouth, arriving there at 05.35. Having located a transport café within the town and sated my hunger with

This was my first photograph taken with the Kodak Colorsnap 35 given to me by my parents as a birthday present that January. The 06.35 Weymouth to Brockenhurst (via the Castlemans Corkscrew original main line route from London to Dorset), with Bournemouth allocated BR 4MT No. 76026 in charge, calls at Wimborne on 25 April 1964 – just a week before the line's closure. The Mogul was luckier in surviving until the end in July 1967.

a breakfast, I departed at 06.35 with sister No. 76026 which back-tracked over the entire route just covered via Wimborne – formerly an important railway junction with the S&D and nowadays a thriving market town – as far as the West Moors before continuing to the 'capital' of the New Forest – Brockenhurst.

This particular line was known by local railwaymen as the 'Castleman's Corkscrew' so nicknamed after Wimborne solicitor Charles Castleman, one of the leading campaigners for the construction of the route and its wandering nature. This line was the original route from London to Dorchester and because the landowners in the Bournemouth area did not want the intrusive railway to traverse their lands, they forced the railway builders to circumnavigate their estates accordingly. In 1870 the same landowners relented, having subsequently realised they were losing out on the money from both business and tourism that the railways naturally brought with them and a line was built from a junction at Ringwood (nowadays a town of such a size it has its own bypass) via Hurn and Christchurch to Bournemouth. Eighteen years later a more direct cut-off route via New Milton was constructed, relegating the original route, being covered by myself that glorious spring morning, to the status of a feeder line. With the wonderment of the ever-changing newly discovered scenery which I was passing through, the lack of sleep on these complicated intensive itineraries never seemed to catch up with me until later in the day! A third Bournemouth resident of the same class of locomotive, this time No. 76069, was to work my next train – the 09.29 via the 'new cut-off' through the New Forest the 15 miles to Bournemouth. These BR Standard Mogul locomotives were a textbook example of the free steaming maids of all work that had proliferated most of BR (the Southern in particular) during the 1950s. The now-familiar rasping sounds from the front end did not appear to disturb the deer and ponies grazing near to the line, and the animals were obviously well used to the staccato exhaust from the trains when starting off from the many intermediate stops en route.

Bournemouth, in those days, was privileged to have had two railway stations – the Central, at which I changed trains, remains today but the West, from which my Bristol-bound train was to depart, was closed under the 1967 electrification scheme, the land of which was used for the new electric units maintenance depot. With no suitable connection to get me to the West station, I caught a Weymouth-bound train to Poole where I connected onto the 11.40 Bournemouth West to Bristol Temple Meads – in charge of which was the subsequently preserved venerable then thirty-seven-year-old Templecombe-allocated No. 44422. Over 500 of these versatile 0–6–0 Fowler-designed freight locomotives were built between the wars and, resulting from the origins of the route, ex-LMS locomotives penetrating deep into Southern territory was not that unusual. The incongruous mix of ex-LMS locomotive and Southern malachite green Bulleid stock was therefore often the norm.

Just managing to get a corner seat on the crowded train, I sat back and looked forward to the 1½-hour journey ahead. The freight locomotive appeared to have no trouble with this 'light load' of four vehicles and kept time without a problem, calling at only the most important stations along this Stour valley route – one of which was Blandford Forum (initial terminus of the Dorset Central railway in 1860) where we crossed with a southbound service. The gradient steepened from this point and with 5ft 3in driving wheels and a certain identifiable difference about the exhaust from anything I had previously heard on Southern metals, we arrived on time at the wonderfully named, well kept and beautifully adorned (with flowers)

The axis of the Somerset & Dorset was here at Evercreech Junction when on 25 April 1964 Templecombe-allocated ex-LMS 4F No. 44422 departs with the 11.40 Bournemouth West to Bristol Temple Meads. Although withdrawn at Gloucester the following May, she fortunately made it into preservation.

Templecombe-allocated ex-GWR 3MT 0–6–0 No. 2218 performs shunting duties at Highbridge on 25 April 1964 having just brought me the 22 miles over the Somerset Levels from Evercreech Junction. Withdrawn that November, services over the final months of the branch's existence were monopolised by Ivatt 2MTs.

Yeovil-allocated ex-SR U Mogul No. 31792 stands at Taunton with the 16.25 departure for her hometown on 25 April 1964. The line was closed the following June – the Mogul being withdrawn four months later.

Evercreech Junction. I changed there onto the 13.15 departure for Highbridge which, that day, had one of Collett's 3MT 0–6–0s in charge – No. 2218. Also a Templecombe-allocated locomotive she was looking very sorry for herself with rust and grime everywhere and all identifying numberplates removed or missing. When the S&D was originally constructed, this section I was about to travel over was the main line – a fact I found hard to believe as the one-coach, one-van train trundled along taking 45 minutes for the 22 miles – travelling over the Somerset Levels part of which is now the site of the famous Glastonbury Festival. It was as if the line was run as a family concern with all the railwaymen acknowledging each other in friendly terms and little sense of urgency. Just three trains per day over this section were not exactly inspirational to prospective customers – and sure enough travellers were few and far between.

I then made a quick hop along to Taunton where, expecting a DMU, one of Maunsell's Moguls, Yeovil-allocated No. 31792, was waiting with the 16.25 Yeovil departure. A combination of lacklustre scenery while crossing the Somerset Levels (again!) and tiredness finally lead to the inevitable eye closure. Having slept through the Town station, where I had planned to alight for the shuttle to the main line station of Yeovil Junction, I quickly backtracked from the Pen Mill station to Town and caught the two-coach rail-motor (WR terminology for push-pull) shuttle to the main line station at Yeovil Junction being worked by another of Collett's designs – this time 0–6–0 pannier tank No. 6412. This enabled me to catch a stopping service to Templecombe that conveniently connected into the last London-bound train. Arriving back into Waterloo at 22.08 (1964 was the changeover year from 12- to 24-hour timings within the travel industry) I calculated the cost of the outing, fares only, as 26s. That was a big chunk of my £4 per week wages – my travels were to increase only as my earnings rose!

Time	Station	Traction	Name	Miles
arr – dep				
01.15	Waterloo	34096	*Trevone*	
02.57 – 03.17	Salisbury	76055		83¾
05.35 – 06.35	Weymouth	76026		58
08.50 – 09.29	Brockenhurst	76069		50½
10.05 – 10.40	Bournemouth Central	76025		15¼
10.49 – 11.51	Poole	44422		5¾
13.02 – 13.15	Evercreech Junctionn	2218		40¾
14.02 – 15.05	Highbridge	D7091		22¼
15.35 – 16.25	Taunton	31792		18
17.37 – 17.45	Yeovil Pen Mill	82044		26
17 47 – 17.50	Yeovil Town	6412		0½
17.54 – 18.29	Yeovil Junction	34084	*253 Squadron*	1¾
19.05 – 19.28	Templecombe	34096	*Trevone*	10½
22.08	Waterloo			112¼

Total mileage = 445¼

5

VICTORIAN TANKS RETIRED

By 1964, the Dugald Drummond-designed 0–4–4 tank locomotives, 105 of which were built between 1897 and 1911, were eking their final days out at Bournemouth depot. Originally utilised on Waterloo suburban services resulting from the inexorable spread of electrification, most had been dispatched to secondary line train services throughout the Southern Railway/Region from Kent to Devon – excepting the one which fell down the lift shaft to the Waterloo and City line in 1948! Because of their age it had been decreed that no further overhauls were to be undertaken and as and when repairs became necessary, they were to be withdrawn. Utilised on shunting duties at both of Bournemouth's stations they also worked the 'push-pull' services on the Lymington and Swanage branches – no other locomotives being adapted to perform what was by then becoming a rarity of train operation. Having learned only days earlier from my manager Les that the remaining nine were being withdrawn on the following Monday, he released me half an hour early from my Saturday morning shift (part and parcel of railway clerical duties in those days) in order to catch the 11.30 Bournemouth departure on a brilliantly sunny Saturday 9 May. In reality the wholesale slaughter was amended to 'to be withdrawn upon failure' thus extending their stay of execution merely by a few days, the diktat being accomplished by the end of the month!

After an uneventful 93-mile journey with 'West Country' No. 34004 *Yeovil*, upon arrival at Brockenhurst I crossed platforms for the 13.52 'push-pull' departure to Lymington Pier at the rear of which fifty-nine-year-old M7, No. 30052, was impatiently waiting for the off. This scenic and attractive 5¼-mile branch line, opened in 1858, passes through the sparsely populated Setley plain virtually devoid of trees bordering the eastern edge of the New Forest, to the delightful town of Lymington from which ferries ply across the Solent to the West Wight resort of Yarmouth. Passenger numbers, until the early 1960s, warranted through-trains from London on summer Saturdays just to cope with the then thousands travelling by rail to the island. Nowadays, with the greater car usage causing tailbacks through Lyndhurst to the M27 turn-off, a shuttle service is deemed sufficient. This was my first visit along the line – little did I know that over the next three years whenever I espied a 'required' tank while passing through on a main line train, I would leap off and catch it. By adopting this strategy I eventually travelled with Bournemouth's entire stud of Ivatt 2MT 2–6–2Ts and Standard 4MT 2–6–4Ts. On one Sunday afternoon in January 1967 two return trips within two hours were undertaken when the changeover on the Lymington branch at 16.30 yielded two Ivatts – No. 41295 and the now preserved No. 41312. The dubious distinction of being Britain's last steam-worked branch line ended on Sunday 2 April 1967 with three-car Hampshire diesel units taking over the following day – themselves being displaced several months later by electric units. I only learned some years later that steam services would have remained on the branch until that July but the Lymington men qualifying for redundancy opted not to accept any date other than that already agreed between BR and ASLEF – that being the original electrification date! I was aboard several rail tours which subsequently visited the branch, always topped and tailed (engine at both ends) – the train-lengths precluding running round at the Pier station. When the slam-door EMUs became displaced throughout the Southern Region in the late 1990s, South West Trains cleverly obtained a heritage status for the branch, thus enabling them to operate (albeit with central door locking installed) under a special remit authorised by the Health and Safety Executive. With the supply of replacements parts becoming scarce they were eventually withdrawn in 2010, being supplanted by more modern sliding-door stock.

Anyway, I digress. Returning to my May 1964 trip, as perhaps befitting her age the asthmatic-sounding locomotive, no doubt in a run-down condition, temporarily stalled on the slight incline along the main line just before the branch junction but, with a reduced turnaround time at Lymington Pier, I arrived back into Brockenhurst on schedule a mere thirty-four minutes later. With the first objective having been accomplished I continued down the line to Bournemouth en route to the second objective – the Swanage branch. Deliberately positioning myself in the rear of the 12.35 Waterloo to Weymouth service, it changed locomotives upon detachment at Bournemouth Central station from 'Battle of Britain' No. 34077 *603 Squadron* to Standard Mogul No. 76069. This neatly connected into the 15.40 departure for Bristol which, on that day, had No. 73051 in charge – one of the stud on Bath Green Park's Standard Fives. The Western Region, always having a predilection for being different to the rest of BR, often embellished their Standard locomotives during their overhauls with a Brunswick green livery resulting, in my opinion, in an aesthetically pleasing enhancement to an already handsome high running-plated design.

Changing at the cramped sharp-curved station at Poole onto the 13.30 Waterloo to Weymouth for the 7-mile journey to the Swanage branch junction of Wareham, I caught my first 'Merchant Navy' class locomotive – No. 35027 *Port Line*. If anyone

Preparing to propel the 13.52 departure out of Brockenhust over the 5¼-mile branch to Lymington Pier on 9 May 1964 was fifty-nine-year-old ex-LSWR 0–4–4T M7 No. 30052. All remaining nine examples of this class were withdrawn before the month's end.

Twenty-eight days before her withdrawal and M7 No. 30480 places the Bournemouth West portion onto the rear of a Weymouth to Waterloo service at Bournemouth Central on 25 April 1964.

had said that over the next thirty-eight months I was to accumulate over 17,000 miles behind eighteen examples of this class I wouldn't have believed them – but that was exactly what was to happen!

We now move on to the attractive Isle of Purbeck – which at the time had a branch line running the length of it through to Swanage. These days, the two alternative routes to the Isle of Purbeck are either by the chain-operated Sandbanks Ferry, with its attendant queues for the ferry extending back to Poole harbour, or the A351 via Wareham. Originally proposed for closure in 1968, BR citing a shortage of carriages (diesel units) available to operate the service, vociferous local opposition highlighting inadequate replacement bus alternatives successfully opposed it – but the line did eventually succumb to closure some four years later. It was only the creation of a preservation group and the protection of the trackbed from development (against strong pressure for use as a bypass at Corfe Castle) that has made today's highly successful Swanage Railway possible. With severe summer traffic congestion throughout the isle, a park and ride station adjacent to the A351 at Norden, just north of Corfe Castle, is persuasive enough to entice considerable numbers of Swanage-bound drivers out of their cars. With the attractions of Corfe Castle (National Trust) and the Victorian seaside town of Swanage the railway is on to a winner. The eventual intention of reconnection with the main line near Wareham (Worgret Junction) will effectively reverse the erroneous decision in 1972 to close the line.

Returning to that May visit, waiting in the Down bay platform at Wareham with the 16.57 'push-pull' departure for Swanage was M7 No. 30107 – a representative of the class which had monopolised branch services for well over thirty years. The terminology 'push-pull' is a mode of operation for locomotive-hauled trains allowing them to be driven from either end. A cab was built into the carriage furthest away from the locomotive, which provided the driver with basic controls along with a bell or other signalling code system to communicate with the fireman located in the engine itself. Using this system enabled the driver to instruct the fireman to operate the controls not available in the cab – thus reducing the turnaround times at terminals by the elimination for the need of the engine to run round the stock. With the other branch train that day being operated by a non-auto fitted Ivatt Tank locomotive, I was indeed fortunate in catching an M7. Staying aboard at

My first run with a BR 5MT 4–6–0, Bath Green Park's No. 73051, was on 9 May 1964 while working the 15.40 from here at Bournemouth West for Bristol Temple Meads. It's all gone! The locomotive was withdrawn in August 1965, the station closed in October 1965 and services over the line which she was to travel that day ceased in March 1966.

The subsequently preserved ex-LMS Ivatt 2–6–2T No. 41312 is depicted arriving into Corfe Castle on 9 May 1964 with the 17.00 Swanage to Bournemouth Central. The reduction in requirements in the area, partially caused by dieselisation of the Swanage services in September 1966, resulted in her being transferred to Nine Elms – she being one of that depot's allocation caught by myself during the final months of 'The Kenny Belle'.

M7 No. 30107 sits waiting time at Swanage on 9 May 1964 with the 17.38 departure for Wareham. This station was closed in 1972 but is now the thriving HQ of the Swanage Railway preservation group – whose eventual aim of reconnection with the national network at Worgret Junction is nearing achievement (at the time of writing).

Swanage upon return to Wareham I changed onto a Waterloo-bound train, sitting back and relaxing while listening to the hard-working 'Merchant Navy' at the head of my returning journey to the smoke – satisfied that the day's objectives had been successfully accomplished. All the M7s were withdrawn by the end of that month – but one, No. 30053, somehow survived the cull, went to a museum in the USA and has since returned, working services over its old haunts on the Swanage Railway.

Passenger services on the branch remained steam-operated, by Bournemouth-resourced power of varying classes, until September 1966 when DEMUs took over until closure.

6

GO WEST YOUNG MAN

The term 'Withered Arm' refers not, as readers might have associated it, with one of Thomas Hardy's stories, but a nickname railwaymen gave the railway routes west of Exeter. This referred to how these lines appeared on a map of the L&SWR system in comparison to the dense, largely straight-running main lines of the London suburbs and Hampshire – the sparse network in the west with the single main line splitting into a series of long, wandering, branches resembling a withered limb and fingers. The lines were built to much lower engineering standards than the routes nearer London, with steeper gradients, fewer major bridges, tunnels or cuttings, a lower maximum axle loading and often long stretches of single track. Constructed over a lengthy period of nearly fifty years the final section, between Camelford and Wadebridge, was not completed until 1899.

My first visit to the area was during August 1963 when my parents and brother, travelling by road via the only route then available – the A30 and the notorious Exeter bypass which had opened in 1938 with its attendant 12-mile tailbacks – to Woolacombe, but proudly perhaps showing my increasing independence by making use of my BR free pass facility, I went by train. I joined the very orderly queue at Waterloo winding around the appropriately marked packed concourse, starting under the correct letter as indicated by a large square block suspended from the roof, with everybody staying in line until 'called' forward to board the train – a scenario impossible to envisage in today's frenetic world. After six hours and over 200 miles of steam travel in a Bulleid single compartment, side corridor carriage (reserved seat of course) I arrived at the nearby station of Mortehoe, there catching a local bus for the remaining few miles to rejoin my family. No photographs, no documentation – I will never know what locomotives were at the front. They could even be ones which, come the following year, would be withdrawn!

Regional boundary changes meant that the Western Region had taken over all the lines west of Salisbury during 1963 and, in addition to attempting to be the first region to gain brownie points with the recently government-created British Railways Board to eliminate steam traction, was also planning drastic rationalisation of the newly inherited Southern infrastructure. It was to be the final summer of steam operations on these ex-SR lines and with this in mind I studied the relevant timetables and came to the conclusion that the majority of the 'doomed' lines could be covered in two hits, providing I was prepared to forfeit a night's comfortable sleep in my own bed. So on two consecutive Saturdays in the July of 1964 I found myself on board the 00.45 departure from Waterloo, a summer Saturday relief to the regular 01.10 newspaper service, bound for pastures new. On the first of the two Saturdays, noting that the train was not excessively crowded, I found an empty compartment towards

The front cover of a Carriage Working Notice issued by BR (WR) for train formations throughout the West of England over the ex-SR routes 'awarded' them resulting from the regional boundary changes earlier that year.

The front cover of the local timetable issue that I often referred to during my travels through Devon and Cornwall in July 1964.

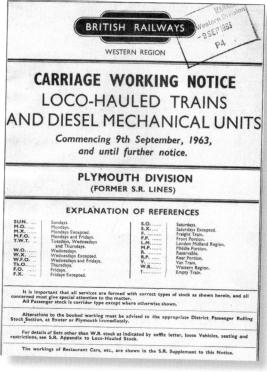

BRITISH RAILWAYS

WESTERN REGION

CARRIAGE WORKING NOTICE
LOCO-HAULED TRAINS
AND DIESEL MECHANICAL UNITS

Commencing 9th September, 1963, and until further notice.

PLYMOUTH DIVISION
(FORMER S.R. LINES)

EXPLANATION OF REFERENCES

SUN.	Sundays.	S.O.	Saturdays.
M.O.	Mondays.	S.X.	Saturdays Excepted.
M.X.	Mondays Excepted.	F.	Freight Train.
M.F.O.	Mondays and Fridays.	F.P.	Front Portion.
T.W.T.	Tuesdays, Wednesdays and Thursdays.	L.M.	London Midland Region.
W.O.	Wednesdays.	M.P.	Middle Portion.
W.X.	Wednesdays Excepted.	R.	Reservable.
W.F.O.	Wednesdays and Fridays.	R.P.	Rear Portion.
Th.O.	Thursdays.	V.	Van Train.
F.O.	Fridays.	W.R.	Western Region.
F.X.	Fridays Excepted.	†	Empty Train.

It is important that all services are formed with correct types of stock as shown herein, and all concerned must give special attention to the matter. All Passenger stock is corridor type except where otherwise shown.

Alterations to the booked working must be advised to the appropriate District Passenger Rolling Stock Section, at Exeter or Plymouth immediately.

For details of Sets other than W.R. stock as indicated by suffix letter, loose Vehicles, seating and restrictions, see S.R. Appendix to Loco-Hauled Stock.

The workings of Restaurant Cars, etc., are shown in the S.R. Supplement to this Notice.

PRICE
6d.

train services· tours· fare tables

15th JUNE to 6th SEPTEMBER 1964

British Railways
WESTERN REGION

PLYMOUTH DIVISION

Go Western

the front of the ten-vehicle train, took the light bulbs out of the roof, drew the blinds, and stretched out for some sleep – only to be admonished by the guard before departure that by performing such an act, fuses (apart from his) could be blown elsewhere in the train. Needless to say, after his departure at Salisbury, I achieved my objective. After a slight delay near Battersea resulting from engineering work (nothing changes!) this multi-portioned train shed some vehicles at Exeter (for Ilfracombe and Torrington) and at Halwill Junction (for Bude) leaving us with just two carriages for the Atlantic coast resort of Padstow.

If the line and service had survived into today's railway just imagine the repetitive and necessarily complicated near continuous automated announcements that passengers would have had to endure – all night long! In an impossible-to-recreate scenario today, this lengthy train had left the capital city in the middle of the night and was now down to a mere two coaches trundling along through the picturesque bucolic countryside of Cornwall before the milkman and postman had delivered, calling at such evocative sounding places such as Egloskerry, Port Isaac Road (location of the *Doc Martin* series) and St Kew Highway. We called at all stations and halts, often waiting time or crossing eastbound services bound for London for this was after all a summer Saturday and with their week's vacation completed (often the maximum quota allowed back then), the holidaymakers were homeward-bound. As we neared the Atlantic coast itself there was a distinctive salty tang on the breeze which upon arriving at Padstow was absent and instead

Unmodified BoB 4–6–2 No. 34054 *Lord Beaverbrook* is seen on 11 July 1964 at a sea mist-shrouded Padstow having worked the 88¼ miles from Exeter with the overnight train from London. This Exmouth Junction-allocated Pacific was withdrawn two months later and the picturesque meandering route she had just brought me over was to close in October 1966.

Merchant Navy 4–6–2 No. 35009 *Shaw Savill Line* prepares to depart Exeter Central on 11 July 1964 with one of the multi-portioned 'Atlantic Coast Express' trains. She never survived the cull of ex-SR steam instigated by the new rulers (WR) two months later.

Ex-GWR 0–6–0PT No. 4694 at Exeter Central on 11 July 1964 having just banked a London-bound service up the 1 in 36 gradient from Exeter St Davids. After deliberately positioning myself in the rear vehicle of said train to enjoy the sound and spectacle of the efforts made by this seemingly diminutive tank locomotive, my hearing only returned to normal some hours later!

of the expected view of the wide sweep of the Camel Estuary, a thick sea mist, a portent of a gloriously hot sunny day, had rolled in, obscuring all.

To the accompaniment of the raucous cries of circling gulls I took the opportunity to stretch my legs around the empty streets of the town, as yet to be invaded by the four Rick Stein restaurants. Not knowing it at the time, this journey proved to be the longest steam-operated 'normal' service I was ever to encounter within Britain – at just less than 7 hours and 260 miles. Once the recipient of up to five services per day from London, including the prestigious 'Atlantic Coast Express', the trackbed between Wadebridge and Padstow alongside the Camel Estuary is now part of an extensive Sustrans network of trails for the usage of both pedestrians and cyclists – as are many such closed lines throughout Britain. With the ever-improving road network, funded by the allegedly impartial road infrastructure company-owning transport minister Ernest Marples, and burgeoning car ownership, both holidaymakers and local residents were making greater use of the far greater flexibility a car could provide and thus deserting the railways in their thousands. Marples did, however, make one concession during early 1964. He stated that no seaside branch lines were to close prior to that October – to allow prospective passengers to plan their holidays in the knowledge that they could complete their journeys entirely by rail! British Railways, always dependent on ever-reducing subsidies from the government were, by the 1960s, past masters in the art of cost-cutting plans often referred to as 'closure by stealth'. In this line's case, to ensure the economic case for retention was based purely on the decreasing passenger usage they diverted freight traffic away from the route and, unbelievably, deliberately omitted to include the line's services in the summer timetable of 1966 (June), fooling any intending passengers into believing the line had already ceased to exist, the actual closure not being implemented until that October.

The second objective of this trip was to visit the three East Devon branch lines (off of the soon to be downgraded ex-SR main line to Exeter) also under the threat of closure – namely to Exmouth, Seaton and Lyme Regis. So rather than retrace my steps via Launceston and Okehampton I caught a local service, worked by North British Type 3 D6323, to Bodmin Road, now Bodmin Parkway, situated on the ex-GWR main line to from Penzance, and returned east to Exeter via Plymouth and the infamous Dawlish coastal route – so often in the news when rough seas swamp the tracks. Back then an alternative to that route in adverse weather conditions was the ability to run trains to the west and north of Dartmoor via Okehampton, but short-sighted economics were the be all and end all and that route was axed in 1968. Typically not actually recording the train details on non-steam services caught, I am unable to remember if it was a Penzance to Paddington or Midlands train. The power was, however, noted – it was Type 4 Hydraulic 'Warship' D814 *Dragon* throughout with assistance up Daignton bank by a second 'Warship', namely D853 *Thruster*. Changing back onto Southern services at Exeter St Davids (a unique station where, to this day, trains to London can depart in both directions as a result of competition between rival companies), I caught a service to the more conveniently located (for the town) Central station. All trains of any length were assisted up the 1 in 36 incline between the two Exeter stations in those days by a banking engine being attached at the rear of it and this day was no different. Travelling in the rearmost vehicle it was some time later that day when my hearing returned to normal having been nearly deafened by the extremely vociferous assistance by a diminutive, but obviously up to the task, nineteen-year-old Swindon-built tank engine 0–6–0PT No. 4694.

Most of the Devon branch trains by that date had gone over to diesel units with one exception – and needless to say with astute planning I was able to travel on it. Catching the 12.45 DMU from Exeter Central along the only East Devon branch that has survived the massacre of lines to Exmouth, I passed Exmouth Junction shed, where the allocation of Pacific locomotives that supplied all the needs for services emanating from Exeter Central (ALL trains changed locomotives there) were based, and travelled alongside the scenic estuary of the River Exe. Exmouth station, subsequently demolished to make way for a 'transport interchange' hub, was also the terminus of a branch from Sidmouth Junction and the 13.34 departure, hauled by locally allocated BR 3MT 2–6–2T No. 82042, was in fact a train with through-vehicles to London Waterloo, which combined upon reaching the main line with a service from the west. My original plans went a bit adrift at this point because – as a result of late running of opposite way workings along the single-track branch via Budleigh Salterton – my train took 65 minutes to cover the 16 miles! All was not lost by the delay, it just meant some minor rescheduling and I now had to travel the 11½ miles along the main line to the next branch line terminus – at Seaton Junction. The 11.48 Plymouth to Waterloo deigned to call at both junction stations and was to prove my only run with 'Merchant Navy' No. 35019 *French Line CGT*. Having passed by the subsequently closed Seaton Junction station in recent years (by road of course) the station still stands as a mute reminder of a previous life, the use of standard SR concrete slabs having stood the test of time. Today the Seaton Tramway uses the trackbed of the branch south of Colyton and offers very pleasant views of both countryside and estuary from the open top deck of a preserved tram and is well worth a visit.

The now preserved Unmodified Pacific No. 34070 *Manston*, working the all stations on the 15.35 Exeter Central to Yeovil Junction train, took me the 3¼ miles further east along the main line to the town famous for its carpet manufacturing industry – Axminster. This was the junction station for the 6¾-branch line to Lyme Regis – nicknamed 'The Pearl of Dorset' due to its picturesque qualities. Arguably one of the finest branch line journeys in southern England, the views from the train could be enjoyed at leisure as a consequence of the line's sharp curves, stiff gradients and weight-restricted bridges. It was restricted to a 25mph maximum, the route having been opened in 1897 (a twenty-two-year delay after the first sod had been cut) resulting from the passing of the 1896 Light Railway Act. Although reports of the line having reverted to steam operation were filtering through, it was not to be and a ubiquitous 'bog cart' was the order of the day. Upon arrival at Lyme Regis another delay ensued while the driver rectified a fault on the diesel unit causing further

Meandering into Seaton Junction with the 15.35 stopping service from Exeter Central to Yeovil Junction on 11 July 1964 is the subsequently preserved Light Pacific No. 34070 *Manston*. These slow all-station services were a total anathema to Beeching who, in his reshaping proposals, successfully closed ten intermediate stations (including this one) along this ex-LSWR main line leaving a two-hourly Waterloo to Exeter semi-fast service calling at the remaining eight.

How can you not be moved by the majesty of a 'Merchant Navy' class locomotive? Little did I know on that day that I was to travel nearly 17,000 miles with nineteen different examples over the next three years – but alas not this one. No. 35025 *Brocklebank Line* is seen departing Axminster on 11 July 1964 with the 15.00 Waterloo to Plymouth/Ilfracombe.

The 16.00 departure for Seaton Junction on 11 July 1964 is seen here at the Devon coastal resort terminus of Seaton. This 4¼-mile branch was closed in March 1966 – some of the trackbed being used by the unique Seaton Tramway.

Lyme Regis (closed November 1965) had a long association with locomotives of the ex-LSWR Adams 0415 4–4–2T class which, by the time of my visit, had long gone. The 17.15 departure for the 6¾-mile journey to the junction station of Axminster on 11 July 1964 was formed of a mundane DMU.

consternation to a tired and weary traveller in case I missed the final train of the day to take me back to London. This was the 16.00 Plymouth to Waterloo which that day had Light Pacific No. 34052 *Lord Dowding* in charge. She was to become a firm favourite of mine and I subsequently travelled with her on her last passenger duty between Winchester and Eastleigh some three years and 1,173 miles later. Indeed, colleagues within the final office of my career wheedled out of me that fact and presented me with a model of her upon my retirement – which is reposing nearby as I write this story.

Time	Station	Traction	Name	Miles
arr – dep				
00.45	Waterloo	34101	*Hartland*	
	Exeter Central	34054	*Lord Beaverbrook*	171¾
07.26 – 08.12	Padstow	D6323		88¼
09.10 – 09.19	Bodmin Road	D814*	*Dragon*	16½
11.41 – 11.47	Exeter St Davids	34054**	*Lord Beaverbrook*	79
11.50 – 12.45	Exeter Central	DMMU		0¾
13.12 – 13.34	Exmouth	82042		10½
14.14 – 14.52	Sidmouth Junction	35019	*French Line CGT*	16½
15.11 – 15.13	Seaton Junction	DMMU		11½
15.25 – 16.00	Seaton	DMMU		4¼
16.13 – 16.25	Seaton Junction	34070	*Manston*	4¼
16.31 – 16.35	Axminster	DMMU		3¼
16.53 – 17.15	Lyme Regis	DMMU		6¾
17.33 – 18.39	Axminster	34052	*Lord Dowding*	6¾
22.08	Waterloo			144 ¾

Total mileage = 564¾

* assisted between Plymouth and Newton Abbot by D853 *Thruster*
** assisted by 4694

The second trip, exactly one week later, found me once again aboard the 00.45 departure from Waterloo. This time I alighted at Exeter St Davids at 04.30 onto a Plymouth-bound service, unfortunately diesel-operated, which took me as far as Okehampton. As on this leg I was heading for the Victorian resort of Bude I had to change trains once more – this time at Halwill Junction. It was now six in the morning and although still grey, the morning glow of dawn promising a fine day was peeking over the surrounding countryside. Compared to the majority of steam locomotives working services over these lines, a relatively young twelve-year-old tank engine, BR 4MT No. 80041, was working the branch connection. Perhaps being a little younger this locomotive survived the cull of steam locomotives later that year and was moved to Somerset – only to meet the grim reaper in March of 1966. As was often the case when travelling overnight, I had arrived into town before its day had begun and wandered the quiet streets, a favoured watering place of the Victorians, viewing the beachfront and the remains of an ancient canal leading into the tidal basin. The 09.00 departure returned me to the junction station of Halwill, a location which epitomised the bucolic image of the 'Withered Arm' stations, being located in the middle of nowhere and created purely for railway purposes with few inhabitants nearby. An hour or so was spent on an embankment in the sunshine watching, but stupidly not photographing, the complicated working arrangements for the various portions being put together to form home-going holidaymakers services back to the smoke.

I was now about to embark on what turned out to be the highlight of the trip – a journey over the ex-North Devon and Cornwall Junction Light Railway on the 10.52

Halwill Junction to Torrington service. Hauled by Ivatt 'Mickey Mouse' 2–6–2T No. 41249, the one-coach train wound its way through the picturesque North Devon countryside stopping at all stations (in reality either several concrete slabs or planks of wood) and level crossings – the latter because all were ungated with the guard having to alight, walk forward, see the train across and then rejoin! Subsequent research revealed that the 20½-mile route, built as late as 1925 essentially for the

Table 48

HALWILL, HATHERLEIGH and TORRINGTON

Miles			am	am SX SO	am SO	pm SX	pm		Miles			am	am	pm SX SO	pm SO
	Halwill — — — dep			1038	1052	6 30				Torrington ... ... dep	6 25	8 52	4 0	4 40
3	Hole .... — — —			1047	11 1	6 39			1¾	Watergate Halt.	6 32	8 59	4 7	4 47
7¾	Hatherleigh — — ...			11 5	1119	6 57			4½	Yarde Halt.. — — ...	6 46	9 13	4 20	
10	Meeth Halt .— — —			1116	1132	7 8			5½	Dunsbear Halt. — —	6†52	9 18	4 25	6
12½	Petrockstow — — ...	7 55	1126	1142	4 37	7 18			7¾	Petrockstow — — ..		9 28	4 34	5 16
14¾	Dunsbear Halt. — — ..	8 4	1136	1152	4 46	7 28			10½	Meeth Halt. — — — ...		9 38	4 44	5 26
16	Yarde Halt.. — — ..	8 10	1141	1157	4 52	7 34			12½	Hatherleigh — — ...		9 48	4 54	5 36
18¼	Watergate Halt.— — ..	8 24	1155	1211	5 6	7 48			17¼	Hole ... — — —		10 8	5 13	5 56
20½	Torrington. — — arr	8 32	12 2	1218	5 14	7 56			20½	Halwill — — — arr		10 18	5 23	6

SO Saturdays only	SX Mondays to Fridays	† Arrival

This was the customer-unfriendly sparse service over the former North Devon and Cornwall Joint Railway offered to the public at the time of my visit. Needless to say Beeching saw to it that the line was closed in March the following year.

After arriving into Bude just minutes earlier and having espied a photographic opportunity on an embankment near the station I ran, with case and camera in hand, hell for leather to obtain this shot. BR Standard 4MT 2–6–4T No. 80042 departs with the 07.58 for Okehampton on 18 July 1964. This Exmouth Junction-allocated tank was withdrawn in January 1965 – the line closing in October 1966.

Halwill Junction on 18 July 1964 witnesses the arrival of ex-SR N 2–6–0 No. 31849 on the 08.10 Wadebridge to Waterloo. Look at the large layout of tracks/infrastructure at this station – built purely for railway-operating purposes, i.e. the combination/ splitting of services between London and the North Cornish resorts of Padstow and Bude. The platform on the right was the preserve of the twice-daily Torrington service. Closure of the entire site came in October 1966 – a myriad of nearby streets however retaining memories of their railway heritage with names such as such as Station Fields, Station High Road and – unbelievably – Beeching Close!

Barnstaple Junction-allocated ex-LMS 2–6–2T No. 41249 rests from her 'exertions' having arrived at Torrington with the one-coach 10.52 ex-Halwill Junction on 18 July 1964. This speed-restricted (maximum 20mph) ex-ND&CJR line, never exceeded two through services a day and was to close in October 1965. The Ivatt Tank fared little better being transferred to Templecombe and withdrawn upon that line's closure in March 1966.

china clay traffic at Meeth (which kept the line open for freight a further fifteen years after passenger services were withdrawn), was classified as a light railway and was subject to a 20mph maximum speed limit thus explaining its 1½-hour schedule. With just two passenger trains per day sometimes becoming mixed (i.e. freight wagons attached) en route, it was hardly likely the line was an attractive proposition to any prospective passengers. Optimistically built to 'open up the area to tourism and help both farmers and the china clay industry', most prospective customers from the largest town en route, that of Hatherleigh, wanting to get to Okehampton, which was 7 miles by road and 20 by the new railway, opted for the most direct route! The author Matthew Engel (*Eleven Minutes Late*) once caught the evening train from Halwill and arrived at Petrockstowe so early (partially because the timetable allowed for unwanted shunting at Hole and Hatherleigh) that the crew played cards for half an hour in the station – and still reached Torrington ahead of schedule! The one-coach SR dual-classed carriage, provided perhaps in the unlikely event of first class usage, was exchanged at Torrington with a WR two-coach set for the remaining 14 miles to North Devon's most populous town of Barnstaple. A visit to Ilfracombe was then made and to reach it the railway had to climb for 5½ miles with over 1 mile at 1 in 40 to the summit at Mortehoe before descending 2¼ miles at 1 in 36 to the Atlantic coast resort itself. Although my train was powered by a five-year-old WR Diesel Hydraulic, these noxious beasts having infiltrated a previously all-steam scene since the old enemy (the WR) had taken over the services, the climb out of Barnstaple still required assistance, provided on that occasion by a thirty-nine-year-old steam locomotive which although seemingly fit for purpose was withdrawn the following month. With Ilfracombe station being located high above the town the 14 minutes I planned to be there proved insufficient to do anything other than return south with a second Hymek diesel the 15 miles back to Barnstaple. At

Barnstaple Junction station, now a Sustrans interchange of cycling/walking routes, the 15.50 Taunton service was in the hands of a former GWR Churchward Mogul and, as its identification was nowhere to be seen with both smokebox and side numberplates missing, I had to ask the driver for its number. He eventually found a chalked reference to it inside the footplate area – it proving to be Taunton-allocated No. 7306. The next 46 miles across Exmoor were, although very scenic, somewhat uncomfortable in that being in the leading former GWR vehicle it not only 'hunted' at speeds over 20mph but also had compartments with very upright 'ribbed' seats, which I likened to being a flea on the tail of a friendly dog. Carriage couplings and springs creaking and groaning in unison with the train's progress we, at one stage, were running twelve minutes late because of late westbound services over the single-track line. Somehow this appallingly kept rust bucket of a locomotive got us to Taunton – unsurprisingly meeting the cutter's torch a mere eight weeks later. With the stations being situated far from the villages and towns they purported to serve, it was only the holiday traffic to Ilfracombe that kept the line going. The end came in October 1966 – excepting a section near Norton Fitzwarren recently opened by the West Somerset Railway as a turning point for its locomotives. After such a bone-shaking journey, the homebound London train was pure luxury – travelling over what was a novelty in those days i.e. CWR (continuous welded rail). Also complicit to the sleep-inducing environment was another factor not encountered over the past few hours – warm, draught-free accommodation.

Time arr – dep	Station	Traction	Name	Miles
00.45	Waterloo	34082	*615 Squadron*	
	Exeter Central	34020	*Seaton*	171¾
04.35 – 05.18	Exeter St Davids	D6310		0¾
05.57 – 06.25	Okehampton	31855		12½
06.53 – 07.00	Halwill	80041		25
07.35 – 09.00	Bude	80041		12½
09.42 – 10.52	Halwill	41249		12½
12.18 – 12.40	Torrington	41249		20½
13.14 – 13.50	Barnstaple Junction	D6321*		14¼
14.41 – 14.55	Ilfracombe	D7095		15
15.34 – 15.50	Barnstaple Junction	7306		15
17.38 – 18.31	Taunton	D1009	*Western Invader*	45¾
21.05	Paddington			143

Total mileage = 488½

* assisted to Mortehoe by No. 31875

Harold Wilson's Labour government was re-elected during 1966 with an increased majority of 4 to 96 seats. One of its unfulfilled manifesto promises was to halt the line closures – however, as can be noted in Appendix III, most of the routes travelled during these two trips succumbed to the 'good' doctor's surgery

Ex-SR N 2–6–0 No. 31875 was caught on camera at Barnstaple Junction while performing Morthoe banking duties on 18 July 1964. She was withdrawn the following month – the North British diesel in the background, steam's replacement in the area, becoming extinct themselves by the end of 1967.

within the following three years. Additionally, alas never covered by myself, the Okehampton to Bere Alston section, part of the erstwhile diversionary route avoiding the troublesome Dawlish sea wall section of the main Penzance line, was dismissively closed in 1968. With a population of over 10,000 at Ilfracombe, the town's line was a surprising casualty, being truncated at Barnstaple in 1970 and finally Okehampton itself in 1972. Just two sections of the 'Withered Arm' network lines remain today. Resulting from a poor network of local roads and the realisation that closure of the impressive Calstock viaduct conveying the line over the River Tamar would cause considerable inconvenience to present-day commuters, the Callington branch, albeit truncated at Gunnislake, from Plymouth has survived – being marketed under the banner of the Tamar Valley Line. The Tarka Line runs from Exeter to the largest town in North Devon, Barnstaple, and perhaps enjoys the best service ever – albeit using cascaded (i.e. displaced from elsewhere in the country) diesel units. While over the years civil servant Dr Richard Beeching became one of the most hated men in politics, one has to realise that he was given the job of turning the heavily loss-making BR into a organisation that, at best, at least covered its costs. With more motorways opening and burgeoning car ownership, although people always wanted a railway nearby they themselves rarely used it – passenger usage dropping dramatically during the late 1950s and early '60s. It was regrettably inevitable that underused services faced curtailment. It is a fact also that the unions' stranglehold of public services often led to strikes, the most prolific and damaging being the two-week 1955 ASLEF stoppage, and the coach companies were always quick to capitalise on such occasions – the alternatives often proving sufficiently attractive for many customers never to return to rail.

The overnight travel westwards every summer Saturday in the early hours is still enacted these days. Where once usage was made of the duplicated and strengthened newspaper and 'Atlantic Coast Express' train services, the holidaymakers now use the M3/A303/A30 roads, racing to avoid the non dual-carriageway sections of the A303 which become gridlocked by 7.00 a.m., and stopping at Devon's Little Chef restaurants waiting for them to open. Not usually being allowed into holiday accommodation until the afternoon, I recommend from personal experience the Sidmouth donkey sanctuary and Seaton tramway as time-killing activities to visit.

7

TICKET TO RYDE

The railways of the Isle of Wight had to cope with an exceptionally high seasonal demand resulting perhaps from the successful marketing of the island as a Holiday/Garden Isle by the Southern Railway. The last section of the system to open was that between Merstone and Ventnor Town in 1900, but with visitors increasingly bringing their own vehicles to the island using the escalating number of car ferries, over a period of fifteen years from 1951 to 1966 the system shrank from 55 miles to just 8. Smallbrook Junction – always only ever in use during the summer, located 71 chains south of Ryde St Johns – has endured many changes over the years being initially merely a location where the two single lines (to Cowes and Ventnor) diverged, having run as parallel separate entities to that point. In 1926, however, signalling alterations were implemented to increase capacity and the lines north thereof became double tracked. The location has subsequently come into its own with a platform provided for passengers wanting to transfer between Stagecoach's ex-London Underground carriage trains on the Ryde to Shanklin services and the volunteer run Isle of Wight Steam Railway which runs services over the closed Cowes branch to Havenstreet and Wootton.

The first of my three visits to the Isle of Wight during the BR era of steam was in August 1964, the month of Britain's final hanging executions, when, having holidayed with my parents and brother at Totland (they returning home to Kent by the Yarmouth car ferry), I caught a bus to the island capital of Newport (endowed these days with the only stretch of dual-carriageway road on the island) and entered into the Victorian time-warp that the railway system then portrayed. Covering both the Cowes and Ventnor branches I acquired runs with five of the 1889 Adams-built O2 0–4–4Ts. These were representatives from a class which were successfully trialled on the island in 1923 and over the following half-century an eventual twenty-three were sent over from the mainland. They subsequently survived two attempts by BR to replace them with displaced BR 3MT 2–6–2Ts from the 84xxx series in the early 1960s. Upon their arrival on the island they had their bunkers increased in size, in order to complete a day's duty without the need to return to shed midway through their service for coal, and were equipped with Westinghouse air brakes. Apart from their old-fashioned looks and panting pumps, each engine bore a nameplate of a location on the island – a feature that, over the years, endeared them to both visitors and residents alike, they proving to be ideal locomotives for the short but intensive workings required of the island services. Spotting all bar two of the remaining locomotives (the miscreants no doubt languishing deep inside the shed at Ryde), contrary to reports that insufficient serviceable locomotives were available, all services that hot and sunny August

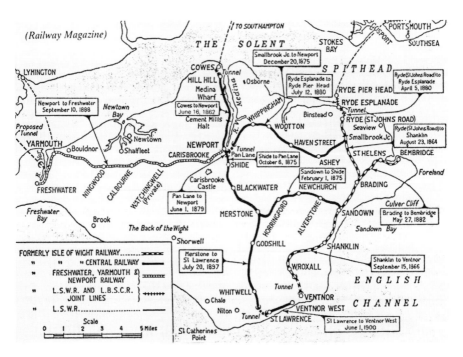

Courtesy of *The Railway Magazine*, a map of the island's once-extensive 55-mile system.

Saturday were running. Taking into account they were all over seventy-five years old and, consistent with BR's finances, were being kept together with a combination of hope and string, all available 'fit' locomotives were pressed into service on such holiday changeover days. My first train that day was the 11.07 departure from Newport and W29 *Alverstone* hissed and panted its way over the first operational (1862) section of railway on the island the 4½ miles alongside the River Medina to the yachting resort of Cowes. This was the most northerly of the island's stations and came to life during the annual regatta held there every summer. Patronage of the island's trains was high during the summer months when the population was swelled by the annual influx of visitors but there was many a day during the rest of the year when trains were running virtually empty.

While at Cowes I witnessed the unique self-shunt engine releasing operation based on gravity of the running lines at the station. Despite there being a crossover at the terminal end between the two main platform lines, summer season trains were often too long to allow the incoming locomotive to take immediate advantage of it. Instead, once clear of passengers, the train would be propelled back a little and braked, the engine then running forward to use the crossover and parallel platform line. The stock would then be allowed to run down the gradient under control of the guard, so that, once at rest and braked, the engine could complete its running round and be coupled on the opposite end. Readers can perhaps appreciate the convenience of today's multiple unit-orientated railway! All of this procedure was dealt with very efficiently and a mere ten minutes later I headed for Ryde with the same engine and coaches. We called again at Newport, which used to have

The traditional picture postcard scene with ex-LSWR 0–4–4T Class O2 W14 *Fishbourne* arriving out of St Boniface Down into Ventnor on 15 August 1964 with the 13.27 ex-Ryde Pier Head. Although one of the oldest – having been constructed in 1890 – she lasted until the end in December 1966.

It's a summer Saturday in August and every available 'fit' O2 was pressed into service to cope with the thousands of holidaymakers streaming across from the mainland in those days before almost universal car-ownership. The 15.20 Ryde Pier Head to Shanklin, with W32 *Bonchurch* in charge, approaches Ryde Esplanade on 15 August 1964 – the adjacent tramway was to close in 1969.

services for Yarmouth (closed 1953) and Sandown (closed 1956), turned east past the remains of stations at the 'royal' Whippingham (for Queen Victoria's holiday home of Osborne House) and Wootton, then called at Havenstreet (nowadays HQ of the IOWSR) and Ashey before passing Smallbrook Junction and alighting at Ryde St Johns Road. I spent the remaining three hours hopping on and off Ventnor line services and, being a summer Saturday, caused all sorts of problems in doing so. Being single compartments and short station stops I didn't have the privilege to ascertain if sufficient room in each compartment had spare empty seats for me, treading on toes and tripping over baggage each time! Everyone was in a holiday mood so no problems were encountered.

And then it was time to leave the island's railway system – a living museum of Victorian engines and Edwardian carriages – and return to the present-day scenario, departing the island on the 16.20 from Ryde Pier Head, crossing the Solent with the resultant cooling sea breeze being a refreshing change from the hot, sultry conditions on the packed steam trains. With little chance of sleep on the bucking bronco of a ride up the Pompey direct (via Haslemere and Guildford) in the 1937-built Maunsell 4 COR unit, it was later that evening that I was reunited with my family at our Kent home.

8

HORSHAM'S
BRANCH LINES

The railway first arrived in the Sussex town of Horsham, famous among real ale drinkers for its now closed King & Barnes brewery, in 1848 with a branch off of the main London to Brighton line at Three Bridges. The branch then became a through-route when it was extended southwards to Pulborough in 1859. The first of Horsham's two 'new' branches was opened from a junction at Itchingfield, some 3 miles south of Horsham, to Shoreham-by-Sea en route to Brighton two years later – with the second, that to Guildford via Cranleigh, being completed in 1865 from a junction even closer at Stammerham. In 1902 a substantial, palatial even, station was constructed just yards south of this point and named Christ's Hospital specifically to cater for the newly relocated (from London) 'Bluecoat' school opened nearby – effectively becoming a connecting junction station between the two branches. The LB&SCR had, however, overlooked the fact that the school only accommodated boarders rather than daily travellers and the seven-platform station became an over expectant white elephant – ironically the present-day two platforms see greater usage.

Taking firstly the 17-mile Guildford branch, which diverged at Christ's Hospital, it was hard to believe that such a quintessential branch line in the true *Oh, Mr. Porter* style could exist so close to the capital. Initially constructed with hope of through-traffic from the Midlands to Brighton, no more than a handful of trains ever serviced it and local patronage was never high. While back in the 1960s the potential commuting population may not have been as large, with Horsham and Guildford a mere 39 and 30 miles respectively from London, the numbers continued to grow in size as London's commuter belt was forever expanding. Throughout the branch's history the train service provided was never one of substance with, during the final two years, only six weekday trains running the entire length between 6.00 a.m. and 8.00 p.m. Normally no service was operated on a Sunday except during the summer, being the routing of excursion trains from Reading (or further west) to Brighton. Built as a light railway, a common method used to keep construction costs down, this meant only certain 'light' weighted locomotives (i.e. Moguls, QIs, etc.) were able to operate these usually lengthy trains. There were no water or coaling facilities over the 45½ miles between Guildford and Brighton and so it was imperative that the locomotives working these usually lengthy trains had adequate supplies of both on board. Although a faded shot of a train at Cranleigh indicated that I had visited the line during 1963, it was on the last Saturday of October 1964

Table 31 — **GUILDFORD and HORSHAM**

Miles	Down	MONDAYS TO FRIDAYS am	am	am	pm	pm	pm	pm	pm	SATURDAYS am	am	am	pm	pm	pm	pm
	78 LONDON Waterloo dep	6 55	7 55	9 50	4 20	5 21	5 50	6 50	7 50	6 55	7 55	9 50	12 50	3 57	4 57	[illegible]
	Guildford 78 dep	8 4	9 8	10 34	5 4	6 5	6 34	7 34	8 34	8 4	9 8	10 34	1 34	5 4	6 5	[illegible]
3¼	Bramley and Wonersh	8 12	9 16	10 42	5 12	6 13	6 42	7 41	8 41	8 12	9 16	10 42	1 44	5 12	6 13	[illegible]
8¼	Cranleigh	8B27	9 27	10 52	5 23	6 24	6 51	7 51	8 51	8B27	9 27	10 52	1 54	5 23	6b29	[illegible]
11¼	Baynards	8 33	9 33	10 58	5 30	6C39		7 58	9B 2	8 33	9 33	10 58	2 1	5 30	6 37	[illegible]
12½	Rudgwick	8 37		11 2	5 34	6 43		8 2	9 6	8 37		11 2	2 5	5 34	6 41	[illegible]
14¾	Slinfold	8 43		11 7	5 39	6 49		8 7	9 13	8 43		11 7	2 10	5 39	6 46	[illegible]
17	Christ's Hospital, West Horsham	8 50		11 14	5 45	6 55		8 13	9 21	8 50		11b20	2 18	5 45	6A56	[illegible]
40½	30 Brighton arr	10 24		12 24	7 27	8 24		9 24	10 17	10 24		12 24	3 24	7 24	8 24	[illegible]
19½	Horsham arr	8 54		11 18	5 50	7 0		8 18	9 26	8 54		11 24	2 22	5 50	7 0	[illegible]
57½	78 London Bridge arr	9 58		1T 7	7T37	8T37		10T 7	11T 7	10T57		1T 7	4T 7	7T37	8T37	[illegible]
57½	78 LONDON Victoria "	10 18		12 40	7 18	8 15		9 40	10 50	10 15		12 40	3 40	7 15	8 15	[illegible]

Miles	Up	MONDAYS TO FRIDAYS am	am	am	pm	pm	pm	pm	pm	pm	pm	pm	pm	SATURDAYS am	am	am	am	pm	pm	pm	pm	pm
	78 LONDON Victoria dep		6§20		1 36		3 36		5 2			6 18			6§20		10 36		1 36		3 36	4 36
	78 London Bridge "		6②24		1T29		3T29		5 14			5 47			6②23		10T29		1T29		3T29	4T29
	Horsham dep	6 46	7 55		3 9		4 53		6 15			7 15		6 46	7 55		12 9		3 9		4 53	6 0
	30 Brighton dep		6 25		2 28		3 58		5 30			6 13			6 29		11 28		2 28		3 28	4 28
2½	Christ's Hospital, West Horsham	6 52	8 0		3b19		4 59		6A24			7 20		6 52	8A 2		12B18		3b19		4 59	6 5
4¾	Slinfold	6 58	8 5		3 24		5 5		6 29			7 25		6 58	8 7		12 23		3 24		5 5	6 11
7	Rudgwick	7 4	8 11		3 29		5 11		6 33			7 30		7 4	8 12		12 28		3 29		5 11	6 16
8½	Baynards	7 9	8 16	9 46	3 33		5 15		6 36			7 33		7 9	8 16	9 46	12 32		3 33		5 15	6 21
11½	Cranleigh	7 18	8 25	9B57	3 39	3 49	5 21	5 26	6 44	6 53	7 22	7 39	7 52	7 18	8 25	9B57	12 39	12 49	3 39	3 49	5B26	6A30
16¼	Bramley and Wonersh	7 28	8 35	10 7		3 59		5A38		7 3	7 32		8a 7	7 28	8 35	10 7		12 59		3 59	5A38	6 40
19½	Guildford 78 arr	7 35	8 42	10 14		4 6		5 45		7 10	7 40		8 15	7 35	8 42	10 14		1 6		4 6	5 45	6 47
49¾	78 LONDON Waterloo arr	8 27	9 29	10 56		4 56		6 47		7 59	8 46		8 56	8 27	9 47	10 56		1 56		4 56	6 47	7 46

Down	Sundays	Up	Sundays
78 LONDON Waterloo dep Guildford 78 dep Bramley and Wonersh Cranleigh Baynards Rudgwick Slinfold Christ's Hospital, West Horsham 30 Brighton arr Horsham arr 78 London Bridge arr 78 LONDON Victoria "	NO SERVICE	78 LONDON Victoria dep 78 London Bridge " Horsham dep 30 Brighton dep Christ's Hospital, West Horsham Slinfold Rudgwick Baynards Cranleigh Bramley and Wonersh Guildford 78 arr 78 LONDON Waterloo arr	NO SERVICE

② Second class only
* Change at East Croydon
§ Second class only. Change at Sutton

A Arr 3 minutes *earlier*
a Arr 4 minutes *earlier*
B Arr 5 minutes *earlier*
b Arr 6 minutes *earlier*
C Arr 7 minutes *earlier*

T Second class only. Change at East Croydon

For OTHER TRAINS between Christ's Hospital and Horsham see Tables 28 and 30

The sparse service on offer over the Horsham to Guildford branch during its final days in 1965.

that I set forth on the 13.34 (SO) departure from the Surrey cathedral city with 'Mickey' Tank No. 41294 in charge. I had, before boarding the train, 'bashed' the shed, conveniently situated off the end of the platform and seemingly cut out of the adjacent chalk cliff. Avoiding the wrath of the foreman, well known for sending spotters out on their ear, I managed to take a few photographs; the position of the sun and the shadows from the cliff always posing a problem – the present multi-storey car park not so deserving of such a need! After what can best be described as a very pleasant journey through the autumnal countryside on the Surrey/Sussex borders was enjoyed, upon arrival at Horsham there was sufficient time before the return journey to walk to and from the shed which was disappointingly void of any action. Taking that into consideration I was very surprised, upon returning to the station, to see a different locomotive, 'Mickey' No. 41299 with the returning 15.09 service! For many years the services had been operated by the ageing M7s and push-pull sets but by the mid-1960s it was monopolised by these Ivatt-designed ex-LMS 2–6–2 Tank engines – the service being sparse enough not to warrant regular attention from me. Nicknamed 'Mickey Mouse' Tanks resulting from their cheerful chuckling noise from the front end, they 'shuffled' along the route day after day – the only stations en route making any attempt to cover their costs being Bramley and Cranleigh. There were 'extra' short workings from Guildford to one of the crossing points en route – Baynards. These were the morning 09.46 from Baynards, presumably to attract shoppers to the cathedral city and to fill an otherwise seven-hour gap in services, and the other was the evening 18.34 train ex-Guildford in an attempt to cater for London commuters. The wonderful scenic countryside en route was fully appreciated courtesy of the low line speed prevailing throughout and the wide-windowed Bulleid vehicles, which provided adequate observational opportunities.

With the announcement of the line's closure in June 1965 (the permanent way having been relaid throughout earlier that year!) an evening visit to the 'commuter' train service was hastily convened during the penultimate month. With three locomotives required for an 'SX' service I had high hopes for an often reported 'Coffee Pot' (Bulleid Q1 0–6–0 freight locomotive) to be utilised, but instead two examples of the normal diet of Guildford's allocation of 'Mickey Mouse' Tanks (41287/99) were in circulation, the third's number not being noted. How useful it would have been to the present-day population, apart from being more environmentally friendly, by keeping all those cars off the roads, if the 8 miles north of Cranleigh (the busiest station on the line) had been retained. Would the retention of this line have helped to keep Guildford's chronic rush-hour congestion down to manageable proportions? There is hope because the authorities have 'protected' the route, currently part of the 37-mile Downs Link footpath, from development and a recent government-appointed quango (ATOC) highlights Cranleigh as one of Britain's twenty towns they wish to see reconnected to the rail system. Wiser after the event comes to mind!

With the cessation of the Horsham services, Guildford's locomotives only passenger work was one rush hour working from Basingstoke to Waterloo and return which their recently acquired (replacing an ageing ex-SR fleet of Moguls) allocation of Standard 5MTs monopolised.

Now to the other branch line from Horsham, the 18 miles – unusually, for a secondary route, double tracked along the Adur Valley – from Itchingfield to Shoreham-by-Sea. In comparison with the aforementioned Guildford branch this line was better served by an hourly all stations service but the case for closure was still made – albeit by a deliberately biased calculation of the passenger traffic. Only the tickets sold by the booking offices on the line were used in the computation of receipts and NOT the incoming, far more substantial, passengers. In April 1964 I embarked on a trip, with my Kodak Colorsnap 35 (a misnomer perhaps – colour film being beyond the finances of a teenage junior clerk's wages!) to photograph

The epitome of a country station albeit only an easy 40-mile commute from London on a sunny evening in May 1965. Guildford-allocated Mickey Tank No. 41299 pauses at Baynards on 19 May 1965 with the 18.05 Guildford to Horsham service. The line was to close the following month with the locomotive transferred to Eastleigh from where she would be withdrawn in October 1966.

An earlier shot of the same Ivatt when she was allocated to Brighton is seen here at Hove when she arrives there on 28 April 1964 with the 11.37 Brighton to Horsham service. Dieselisation of the hourly services along the Adur Valley the following month resulted in the tank locomotive being transferred to Guildford.

A group of us sheared away from the steam-infested ex-LSWR main line at Southampton on Sunday 6 March 1966 to visit the Shoreham to Horsham line on its last day. Unusually for a branch line, double-tracked throughout, this is Southwater – one of the many stations en route at which some of us alighted and purchased souvenir tickets; others holding the doors open for them.

the trains prior to their replacement by diesel units in the following month. The weather was, however, abysmal and I aborted the plan, merely photographing two of them at Hove and Shoreham-by-Sea from either the comfort of platform shelters or through the window of an electric train. The last day of service was Sunday 6 May 1966 and I started my journey out of Waterloo with 'Battle of Britain' No. 34097 *Holsworthy* on the 10.30 to Southampton. Resulting from engineering works the train was diverted via Effingham Junction and Fareham and, judging by 'Joe public' along the lineside, it was obviously a rarity to witness steam-hauled express services traversing the backwater of the Guildford New Line. Retracing some of the route just covered we, a collection of like-minded degenerates, caught the 15.42 DEMU out of Shoreham-by-Sea to Horsham. Calling at all stations including Steyning, Partridge Green and West Grinstead, doors were held open while others visited station booking offices (those open), purchasing souvenir platform tickets and buying up any pre-BR era printed card tickets. My own purchases were subsequently exchanged for Beatles and Rolling Stones LPs upon joining civilian life – the cessation of steam made our hobby redundant.

Horsham station nowadays, having been rebuilt in 1938 as part of the mid-Sussex electrification, is an important transport hub with commuters driving miles in from localities these two long-deceased branches could have served. The town planning authorities are striving to maintain the surrounding countryside from developers intent on plugging the gap with the inexorable encroachment of its large neighbour of Crawley and had these branches survived they might have played a part in distributing the masses!

9

THE NORTH DOWNS LINE

The chapter title alludes to the current marketing logo of the Reading to Redhill via Guildford route, part of which parallels the ramblers' paradise of the Surrey Hills through which any railway construction engineer had to burrow through if constructing a line from London to the south coast. The line's strategic importance was most recognised when, with the London rail network being consistently breached by Luftwaffe attacks during the Second World War, thousands of troops were repatriated from the Dunkirk evacuation on cross-country services avoiding London – returning, together with munitions trains, for the invasion four years later. Threatened with closure in the 1960s, strong opposition by resident influential stockbroker commuters saved the route which, not considered a viable electrification investment, has subsequently settled down to a life as a 'feeder' line into London-bound electric services at Guildford and Redhill and as an alterative route to Gatwick for passengers from the west.

At the time of my first visit (1964) the route had a basic all stations hourly service operated by an amazing variety of steam motive power predominantly resourced from Guildford and Redhill sheds. With nineteen weekday and nine Sunday departures from Reading (South), mainly to Redhill but with some terminating at Guildford and others going through to Tonbridge and even Eastbourne, it was easy to obtain runs with a great many different locomotives from up to seven classes – all in one day. The undulating gradients coupled with frequent stops were nectar to the steam follower, and the constant restarting of the lightweight (most were a mere three vehicles) trains together with wonderful bursts of speed resulting in ear-splitting exhausts – more so from the Standard locomotives rather than the 'mushy' Maunsells – were the norm. The grapevine had activated (before the days of mobile phones and internet which would have made life that much easier) that an exception to the normal diet of Southern-allocated motive power was the 06.50 Reading to Redhill and 11.35 return – they being powered by ex-GWR locomotives.

The novelty value lured me to catch the train on two occasions and, with the Saturday equivalent being diesel, forced me to take some of my precious annual leave – albeit a mere half day on each occasion. I was rewarded with runs with two representatives of the 1938 built 'Manor' class 4–6–0 locomotives – Nos 7813 *Freshford Manor* and 7829 *Ramsbury Manor* – named locomotives on secondary services by that date itself being unusual. I was beginning to appreciate what a rich source of steam haulage was available on the route and, with the impending

Ex-GWR 'Manor' 4–6–0 No. 7829 *Ramsbury Manor* threads her way through Reading (General) station on 7 August 1964 after working into the Southern station with the 11.35 ex-Redhill. Having worked out of Reading on the 06.50 departure that morning the two trains were always WR power resourced and were often homed in upon by enthusiasts wishing a run with ex-GWR locomotives – by that date becoming a rarity. This Swindon-allocated 'Manor' was to be transferred to Gloucester from where she met her fate in December 1965.

Guildford's ex-SR U 2–6–0 No. 31791 arrives into Ash with the two-coach 11.45 Tonbridge to Reading (Southern) on 26 May 1964.

Guildford (70C) was bashed on 31 October 1964 and their 'pet' pilot ex-SR USA 0–6–0T No. 30064 was caught in camera. She became the last steam locomotive to depart the shed on the last day (9 July 1967) destined for Barry but saved for preservation.

dieselisation of the services in January 1965, I 'blitzed' the line with five visits in the preceding few months. I was particularly after the ex-SR 2–6–0 Maunsell 'Woolworths' (so called because a considerable number of components were manufactured at the Woolwich Arsenal to keep the workforce employed after the cessation of the munitions needs from the end of the First World War) for which there would be little work for them after that date and were liable for withdrawal. Of the twenty-two examples remaining, I missed catching runs with only eight – a compensatory aspect being at least I photographed them!

The emphasis on my travels was now changing from route coverage to obtaining as much haulage by as many different steam locomotives as possible and, to this effect, I made thirty-five runs behind twenty-five different locomotives from six different classes, namely N and U Moguls, Q1 0–6–0s together with BR Standard 73xxx 4–6–0s, 76xxx 2–6–0s and 80xxx 2–6–4Ts. Although there still remained a couple of 0–6–0 Q class freight locomotives they appeared to be confined, at least at the time of my visits, to shunting and parcel services. Despite missing out on a run with them, there is still hope because the Bluebell Railway is in the process of restoring one to working order!

Utilising the almost hourly frequency of the passenger service, and a growing appreciation of locomotive diagramming, by basing myself at Guildford and only travelling on trains being operated by 'required' locomotives, the most visited stations were Betchworth, Gomshall & Shere, Shalford and Wanborough, changing over from eastbound to westbound services or vice versa as required. The line had always been at the lower end of priority as regards provision of resources, and both locomotives and rolling stock provided were not always in the best condition, having been displaced or cascaded from elsewhere. The shed foreman often utilised visiting locomotives from other depots and examples from Nine Elms, Eastleigh, Feltham and even Oxley (Wolverhampton) were sometimes caught. The latter catch was a complete surprise. In a dreadful external condition, with front smokebox numberplate missing and dirt covering the driver's side painted number, it was only having alighted from the train at Reading did I find a chalked reference to it on the fireman's side revealing it as Standard Class 5MT No. 73028. It must have been sufficiently healthy internally because she was not withdrawn for a further two years. The aforementioned 'Woolworths' were being withdrawn when failing with the slightest defect and, with nothing else available, Q1 freight locomotives (without any steam heating apparatus for passenger comfort) were sometimes pressed into service. These powerful and unconventional-looking locomotives were nicknamed 'Coffee Pots', their chimney and boiler resembling one, being constructed during the Second World War with the minimum of enhancements – metal being prioritised for the war effort.

The only double-headed train I caught (probably a balancing move to get a spare locomotive from one depot to another) along the line was on my last train of my last visit with two 76xxx engines in charge. A double delay was encountered with this train when not only did it stop additionally at a level crossing to change over keepers, but also at Gomshall when a passenger clearly did not read one of the frequently issued train service supplements to the public timetable which showed the train to NOT be calling there! Little did I realise, at the time, that twenty years hence I would be compiling train crew diagrams and negotiating with ASLEF and NUR representatives in respect of duties and rosters for train crews working the line. This route, whose intermediate stations surprisingly survived the Beeching

A wet and miserable day, 19 December 1964, sees Brighton's No. 80089 arriving into Gomshall & Shere with the 11.05 Reading (Southern) to Tonbridge service. She was to end her working days at Nine Elms in October 1966.

Withdrawn the following day ex-SR Q 0–6–0 No. 30543 'leaks' her way around Redhill yard on 19 December 1964. Never having been hauled by any representative of this freight-orientated class, I am waiting with anticipation the Bluebell Railway's restoration of No. 30541.

Can you feel the cold? Guildford's ex-SR Q1 0–6–0 No. 33006 poses at Redhill on 19 December 1964. Due to the lack of train heating equipment these freight locomotives were only pressed into passenger service when dire shortages of fit alternatives prevailed – I caught two that month!

axe, now has a regular service from Reading to Gatwick – an alternative to the nearby increasingly busy M25. The delightful scenery, with the North Downs never seemingly out of view east of Guildford, is a reminder of what Churchill described as worth fighting for when standing at his Chartwell window while plotting the D-Day invasions.

10

GOING CUCKOO

The secondary route from Tunbridge Wells via Eridge, Hailsham and Polegate to Eastbourne was opened in 1880 by the LB&SCR because it had noted that a large part of Sussex remained without rail transport and was built essentially to ensure that its arch rival, the SER, didn't jump in first – such was the rivalry between companies during those railway mania years. Never serving particularly large centres of population, one of them, Heathfield, held a 'cuckoo fair' annually every April where, legend has it, a quaintly dressed old lady always turned up to release, from her basket, the first cuckoo of the spring. The drivers of the trains over this route thus adopted this terminology and always referred to working 'down the Cuckoo' when so doing – and it was forever thus. Although selected for closure within the 'Reshaping of British Railways Act – 1963', it took a while to die – the opposition being perhaps more vociferous than some. The Beeching axe was lethal and the steam locomotive was an inevitable casualty of both the 1955 modernisation plan and the lethargy resulting from the political vandalism rife in the 1960s. Line closures left vast swathes of both beautiful countryside and, more importantly, numerous substantially large towns without rail services. I am certain that, retrospectively taking into account the road congestion throughout southern England, had those lines affected survived into the 1970s (albeit with diesels) they would be now part of a well-used integrated transport network playing its part in reducing road usage.

With the news of its impending closure having been announced and its obvious proximity to my Kent home, I felt duty-bound to revisit this branch during the last painful rites. With steam services having been 'compacted' to Mondays to Fridays the only method of my catching them was to take the yet another half-day annual leave and, in an attempt to travel with as many of the tank locomotives working these services as possible, on the final day of February 1965 I spent seven hours on twelve different trains over the 10¾ miles of line between Tonbridge and Eridge. I am sure the drivers on that Friday were letting the local residents know that it was the last day of steam services because on the sharp climb out of Tonbridge, some parts of which are 1 in 47 through Somerhill Tunnel to High Brooms, the fireworks display and accompanying crescendo of noise had to seen and heard to be believed. From the following Monday, in a typical 'closure by stealth' action by the authorities so often used, the services between Tonbridge and Eastbourne were severed at Tunbridge Wells West, thus causing any through-passengers to change services. This was to ensure that, once all the economics of the line were taken into consideration when the 'final' decision in respect of a line's future was made, the most loss-making section of the route, in this case south of Eridge

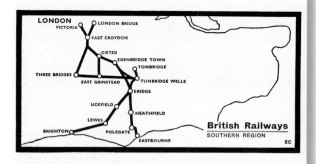

5c

TRAIN SERVICES

between **LONDON** *(VICTORIA & LONDON BRIDGE)*

and **OXTED, EDENBRIDGE TOWN,**

EAST GRINSTEAD, TUNBRIDGE WELLS,

UCKFIELD, HEATHFIELD,

BRIGHTON and EASTBOURNE

From 7th SEPTEMBER 1964 to 13th JUNE 1965
(or until further notice)

The final timetable pamphlet that included the Eridge/Hailsham line – albeit there were many supplementary alterations to it.

which was operated by steam traction (three crew versus two required on a diesel unit) and with antiquated stock requiring replacement, would prove economically unjustifiable – thus signing the line's death warrant.

And so, heavy in heart, a final visit was made to the line that May. The day was hot and sunny and, having caught three other tanks (Nos 80033/88/9) previously that day, as I departed Eastbourne on the 18.01 for my last steam run over the delightful line behind No. 80141 it was with a sadness that was at odds with the weather. As the engine hammered away along the gradient-strewn line at the front of the three-coach train, the sharp exhaust so characteristic of the Riddles-designed handsome tanks resonated throughout the Wealden countryside – covered in all the glory of spring's cloak, it seemingly holding a promise of a great summer ahead. Birds, farm animals, trees – they all had a future ahead of them – but not this railway. Sitting in an armchair-equipped Maunsell open saloon – if ever an idyllic scenario could be resurrected, this has to be it. Economics it wasn't – nostalgia it was! It was just another line closure. The harsh reality of rationalisation witnessing yet more loss of the traditional fabric of country life – as an enthusiast you had to savour each moment while it lasted.

My final visit to the Cuckoo Line was on 11 May 1965 where the BR Standard 2–6–4Ts were in abundance. Coming into Eastbourne behind No. 80088 on the 18.01 arrival I passed (seen here) No. 80034 departing with the 18.00 for Tunbridge Wells West just outside the station. Just thirty minutes later and I headed north with No. 80141 on the 18.31 Eastbourne to Tunbridge Wells West service. This surfeit of steam services merely occurred resulting from the normal 3H DEMUs being put into six- or nine- car formations for the London rush-hour services – Redhill's run-down tanks and some worn-out loco-hauled coaching stock filling the gaps.

But wait, let's bring the story up to date. The Cuckoo trail, a Sustrans/council developed pathway over the former trackbed, now occupies the Polegate to Hailsham section, which is used by considerable numbers of walkers and cyclists. Wooden benches and sculptures adorn the route – made from felled trees from the great storm of 1987. Only limited access to the old route is available north of Hailsham but part of it, Heathfield Tunnel, was repaired and restored in 1997. Often visiting the area by road you can stand on part of the disused trackbed and I sometimes linger awhile and imagine a train along what is now a cycle path. Rotherfield station has been tactfully preserved, having been converted into a holiday home complex with a sunken garden and pond on the orignal trackbed between the platforms. A preserved railway, the Spa Valley Railway, has been established at Tunbridge Wells where the LB&SCR's grandly designed West station has had a conservation order placed upon it and is now a pub/restaurant. The railway has gone from strength to strength and has now extended their area of operations down to the original junction station with the Cuckoo Line – at Eridge. Several attractions such as Groombridge Place Gardens with its 'enchanted forest' and Ashurst forest, play area of A.A. Milne's Winnie the Pooh characters, are nearby. For the more able the station has been reopened at High Rocks, which, by definition, gives access to a local climbing area. The next generation can enjoy a trip along part of line referred to in the above paragraphs courtesy of a dedicated band of volunteers– please support them by taking a trip along the 6-mile line.

11

THE CHASE IS ON

Towards the autumn of 1964 I had begun to realise that the SR steam fleet was diminishing at an alarming rate. So I commenced, the objective being to travel with as many different steam locomotives as possible, what was to become in effect a 'commute' out of Waterloo during the evening rush hour. An entry made in my notebook on 22 September 1964 read, 'this trip is the first of many – the idea being to bump up my steam mileage during the winter months.' Little did I realise that the seed for a nightly 'fix' of steam travel was sown – leading me to accumulate over 43,000 miles behind ninety-one (so far) of Bulleid's Pacifics alone.

Throughout steam's reign I was proud to claim that I NEVER travelled in or out of Waterloo with a diesel. With the scarcity of steam services towards the end, it was quite difficult to avoid the diesels – sometimes having to take a stopping EMU to Alton and travel over the 'Alps' (the secondary route over the North Downs) with a DEMU just for a one-way steam trip back into London! At first it was a weekly visit to Woking then twice weekly then a double trip – out on the 17.09 departure, returning on the 18.26 arrival only to set out once more on the 18.54 departure returning finally on either the 20.25 or 20.36 arrivals. With seven (nine on Fridays) steam services departing Waterloo between 17.09 and 18.54 and fed up with continually having to suffer long queues for tickets at the Waterloo booking office, sometimes missing the train itself, I eventually lashed out on a season ticket for Basingstoke. During the manic height of my travels (September 1966 to April 1967) I had it extended to Southampton. Costing 10s per week (privilege rate) I ensured that I got my money's worth by utilising it on overnight services most weekends together with Sunday excursions during that final winter. With a band of like-minded colleagues we regularly collected at Waterloo every evening to catch the various steam services to Woking, Basingstoke, Andover or Southampton. Very rarely were we all together but our paths often crossed and with information exchanged we continued on our different ways, chasing our own individual locomotives for the magic 1,000 miles.

Visits to works or failures sometimes made particular locomotives temporarily unavailable to us and, God forbid, liable to be condemned when just short of our own personal attempt for that elusive target. My own personal best month for steam mileage was September 1966 during which I accumulated 4,864 steam miles (average of 162 per day) – not bad going for someone whose home was geographically located nowhere near the route involved! Stored deep in my loft, I have all the runs and statistics from those days – I considered including them within this book but it would to be of such length and detail that I might lose the readers' interest! Suffice it to say

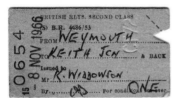

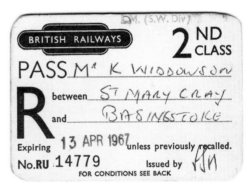

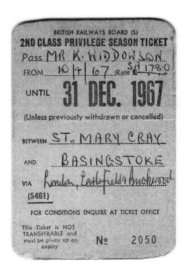

Some of the tickets I used for my travels during these halcyon years.

that towards the end of steam operations if awoken from sleep en route, whether day or night, I would be able to pinpoint precisely where I was by listening to the rail beats or sound of the engine without the need to look for a clue from the passing environment. Obviously being SR-based I had an allegiance to services operated therein – but there were a few of us with LNER or LMS tendencies. Debate as to which company's locomotives were the best, often fuelled by pints in railway taverns at Basingstoke while enduring the ever-increasing gaps between steam services, led to many 'agree to disagree' moments. We (the SR devotees) quietly acknowledged that with THEIR locomotives, by then having almost disappeared, they were on OUR territory and, if they didn't like it they could *go away*.

Lines were closing and steam was in retreat throughout Britain and you couldn't be everywhere on all the many occasions that 'last' scenarios were being enacted. You had to choose which were the most important to yourself – and listen to others ranting on about 'you should have been there!' Steam services on the SR were, in comparison with other modes of traction, somewhat sparse towards the end and, unused to such frequent sightings, the impression upon arriving at major stations such as Crewe, Preston and Carlisle, where steam was still predominant, was breath-taking. At those locations the gradual dieselisation of services, rather than a wholesale changeover, lulled one's sense of the creeping inevitability of the end to a false hope that steam might last longer elsewhere.

The two most travelled-on services

These were the 17.09 (SX) Waterloo to Basingstoke (109 occasions) and the 18.38 (EWD) Salisbury to Waterloo (102 occasions). Taking the 17.09 train first, while the other commuter services were changing over to diesel haulage with either Crompton or Brush traction, this heavily loaded ten-coach commuter train remained) excepting a couple of isolated occasions in August 1966) steam-operated until just five weeks before the end – succumbing then to Type 3 diesel haulage. With a schedule of thirty-one minutes for the non-stop 24½ miles to Woking, it was sometimes difficult to achieve because of the inner suburban intensity of service with the resultant signal checks coupled with substandard coal and the poor condition of the engine. Footplate rides were sometimes offered and gratefully accepted between Farnborough and Hook – i.e. out of sight of any 'official' who usually only frequented the main stations. The leading coach of the train was often a FO (First Open) and much to the annoyance of several bowler-hatted businessmen we all used to hang out of all available windows to, in addition to viewing what was on the way up from the exit road at Nine Elms, observe the signals and soak up the atmosphere of a steam engine working hard. Years later a senior manager at Waterloo said to me (myself having subsequently become a manager) that he recognised me from somewhere and hadn't we met before. Perplexed to begin with, when he mentioned that he lived at Farnborough I realised, but feigned ignorance, that he was one of the many first class passengers who had frequently told us to 'clear off out of here!'

During 1965 the 17.09 was rostered for a 70D (Eastleigh) 'West Country'. This engine was off that morning's 09.39 arrival so I tried to arrange any 'gophering' duties required of me so that I could witness its arrival in order to plan that evening's activity. The fastest start to stop Waterloo to Woking I recorded was on

A beautiful sunny evening in June 1966 and Salisbury's clean Light Pacific No. 34015 *Exmouth* stands at the head of the 17.41 commuter service for Salisbury. Meanwhile, departing from platform 11, No. 34071 *601 Squadron* with the 17.30 for Bournemouth Central. Between 17.00 and 18.30 we had a choice of seven steam departures to travel out on and depending on our needs – mileage accumulation, requirements, fast driver, etc – we sometimes dispersed accordingly, meeting up either later that evening or the following day and exchanging notes and information as appropriate.

24 March 1966 with 'Battle of Britain' No. 34071. Passing Hampton Court Junction in 16 minutes 22 seconds (according to the working timetable it ought to have taken 18½) at 62mph (the max en route), we arrived in 26 minutes 21 seconds (not the 31 minutes the WTT suggested). For one week in May 1967 Light Pacific No. 34052 was allocated the entire week and with Driver Evans (Nine Elms) we had some spectacular accelerating starts out of Woking perhaps the best being on the Wednesday when, with eleven coaches, he took a mere 8 minutes 33 seconds from Woking up the gradient to milepost 31, passing the 'summit' at 70½mph.

The second train, the 18.38 Salisbury to Waterloo was worked by Basingstoke men to their home depot – being relieved by a Nine Elms crew having worked down on the 17.41 commuter train from Waterloo. Some phenomenal speeds were achieved between Basingstoke and Woking, which have been well documented over the years in numerous publications. Salisbury turned out either whatever they didn't want or as dictated by the DMO Wimbledon office. TOPS (Total Operating Processing System) reporting, which would have shown which locomotive was allocated to whatever train, had yet to arrive on the scene but telephone contact was made every afternoon by a fellow clerk and enthusiast Paul whom I had always thought held the post of 'power assistant'. Many years later I learned that he should have only been dealing with vans and he had undertaken the 'responsibility' for locomotives to the Salisbury train on our behalf! When a known 'keen' driver

BoB 4–6–2 No. 34089 *602 Squadron* slips at Basingstoke while restarting the 18.00 Waterloo to Salisbury on 27 July 1966. Salisbury-allocated locomotives were always the cleanest – sufficient manpower not being available at the other depots.

Having just had a run with my favourite Light Pacific, No. 34052 *Lord Dowding*, on the 17.09 ex-Waterloo, a group photograph was taken after arrival at Basingstoke one May evening in 1967. From left to right: fireman, driver Jim Evans, Les (Lurch) Kent, Paul Howard, Keith (Wild Bill) Widdowson, 'Squire' Huntley, Bob (Doze) Thompson, John Clifford, Lenny Chard, Richard (Joe) Jolliffee and Roger Blundell.

was rostered for the turn then the best mechanically 'fit' locomotive steam engine was directed to work the train – Paul being guided by us puffer nutters.

Every type of non-tank locomotive available was likely to be allocated. Perhaps the most surprising, from the occasions I was on board, was Caprotti Standard 5MT No. 73133 on 18 November 1965 – having visited Eastleigh for attention. A creditable 27 minute 57 seconds from Woking to Waterloo with a maximum of 75mph at Hersham was achieved – even though thick fog was the predominant weather. Upon arrival at Waterloo, having double-checked the accuracy of my number-taking at Woking – where she passed by me upon arrival at a fair speed – I noted the 9H shedplate and made it my task upon reaching home that night to ascertain where on earth she was normally allocated. Her home shed was Patricroft, a suburb of Manchester – this hobby of mine certainly contributed to my geographical knowledge of Britain and, after steam's cessation in this country, Europe as well!

This Salisbury train departed Basingstoke at 19.34 but was often early arriving there – on the Up local. Arriving simultaneously on the Up through was the 15.50 from Weymouth (departure of 19.28) and decisions had to be made each evening as to which locomotive was to be travelled with for those 47¾ miles to Waterloo. Those decisions were based on each individual's personal mileage with whatever turned up or whether the Nine Elms driver on the Salisbury was a good bet for high speeds. No longer will the familiar side rod clank of approaching Bulleids be heard – if only that nightly decision was still available to us nowadays!

As the end of steam approached and with the Weymouth going over to Class 73/TC, coupled with the preceding Channel Island Boat services not starting until high summer, more time was spent in a nearby public house at Basingstoke where, as mentioned earlier, 'you should have been there' or 'have you heard the latest' yarns were exchanged. As an aside a similar scenario was enacted at Preston during 1967/8 whereby a receding number of steam trains meant a greater occupancy of watering holes. Today's binge drinking culture among teenagers could never use the 1955 modernisation plans as their reason, could they!

On one occasion, after arrival at Waterloo, the guard remonstrated with the driver over the rough ride he had had in his brake – reminding him that there was (as was often the case) a 75mph speed restricted van within the formation! Having already showered the crew with congratulations (including a whip round for the Southern Railway's Woking Orphanage) we remained very quiet and kept our stopwatches and notebooks well hidden! Taking into account the locomotives not being in prime condition it was a miracle that runs of such significance being recorded were happening at all.

Overnight travels

By the autumn of 1966, with the news that Eastern Region of BR had become the second to eliminate steam and the steam services into Marylebone had been withdrawn that September, the arrival on the SR of diesels from other regions was surely indicative that steam's reign was coming to an end. After spending the summer weekends elsewhere within Britain, I now turned my attention to compiling some serious mileage chasing on the SR and was often to be found doing overnights on the Southern Region – using the Up Mails (22.13 Weymouth to Waterloo, due 03.48) as sleeping accommodation. Having regularly travelled overnight 'oop

BR 25404/32

TRAIN JOURNAL — PASSENGER, VAN OR EMPTY

Train from **WEYMOUTH** to **WATERLOO**
on **FRI** day, the **23RD** of **SEPTEMBER 1966**

TIME **22.13**

S.T. NOTICE NO. ___

STATIONS OR JUNCTIONS	Line run	BOOKED Arr.	BOOKED Dep.	ACTUAL Arr.	ACTUAL Dep.	ACTUAL Arr.	Mins. late Dep.	TIME LOST Station	Motive Power	Signals	Perm. Way	Other Causes	TIME GAINED At Station	By Driver	Particulars of Delays and Special Occurrences
BROCKENHURST		-	0014		0014	✓						1			THICK FOG
REDBRIDGE		00/29½		00/30½		-						½			
SOUTHAMPTON CEN.		0034½	0121	0036	0123	2	½			1	1				
NORTHAM JUNCTION		01/24		01/28		-						1½			
EASTLEIGH		0132	0140	0137½	0146	6	½								HEAVY MAIL TRAFFIC
WINCHESTER CITY		0153	0156	0201	0206	10	2								THICK FOG
WINCHESTER JCN.		02/01		02/13		-			1			1			
WORTING JUNCTION		02/20½		02/38		-						5½			
BASINGSTOKE		0224½	0229½	0243½	0255	26½						1½			
WOKING		0300	0310	0332	0340	30						6½	2		PARCELS
WEYBRIDGE		0321	0325	0351	0356	31	1								
HAMPTON COURT JCN		03/34		04/05		-						½	1		
SURBITON		0337	0344	0408½	0414½	30½								½	
CLAPHAM JUNCTION		04/00½		04/30½		30									
VAUXHALL		0405	0406	0436	0437	31	1								
WATERLOO		0411	-	0443	-	32	1								

Please TICK applicable BOX

Was LOST TIME TICKET handed to Driver? ☐ Yes ☐ No

HEATING
☐ Full ☐ Half
Satisfactory ☐
Unsatisfactory ☐
Comments ___

LIGHTING
Satisfactory ☐
Unsatisfactory ☐
Comments ___

LOADING OF TRAIN
1st 2nd Brake
¼ ½ ¾ Full

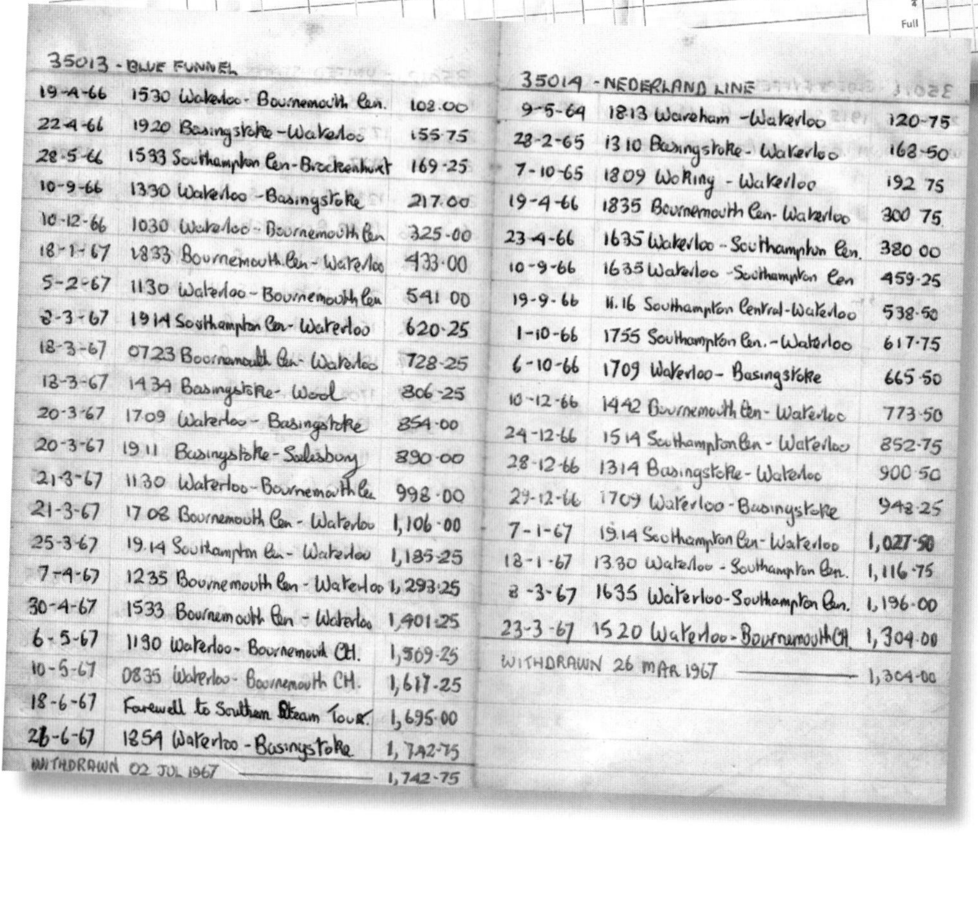

35013 - BLUE FUNNEL

Date	Working	Total
19-4-66	1530 Waterloo - Bournemouth Cen.	108.00
22-4-66	1920 Basingstoke - Waterloo	155.75
28-5-66	1533 Southampton Cen - Brockenhurst	169.25
10-9-66	1330 Waterloo - Basingstoke	217.00
10-12-66	1030 Waterloo - Bournemouth Cen	325.00
18-1-67	1833 Bournemouth Cen - Waterloo	433.00
5-2-67	1130 Waterloo - Bournemouth Cen	541.00
8-3-67	1914 Southampton Cen - Waterloo	620.25
18-3-67	0723 Bournemouth Cen - Waterloo	728.25
13-3-67	1434 Basingstoke - Wool	806.25
20-3-67	1709 Waterloo - Basingstoke	854.00
20-3-67	1911 Basingstoke - Salisbury	890.00
21-3-67	1130 Waterloo - Bournemouth Cen	998.00
21-3-67	1708 Bournemouth Cen - Waterloo	1,106.00
25-3-67	1914 Southampton Cen - Waterloo	1,185.25
7-4-67	1235 Bournemouth Cen - Waterloo	1,293.25
30-4-67	1533 Bournemouth Cen - Waterloo	1,401.25
6-5-67	1130 Waterloo - Bournemouth CH.	1,509.25
10-5-67	0835 Waterloo - Bournemouth CH.	1,617.25
18-6-67	Farewell to Southern Steam Tour	1,695.00
26-6-67	1854 Waterloo - Basingstoke	1,742.75
WITHDRAWN 02 JUL 1967		1,742.75

35019 - NEDERLAND LINE

Date	Working	Total
9-5-64	1813 Wareham - Waterloo	120.75
23-2-65	1310 Basingstoke - Waterloo	168.50
7-10-65	1809 Woking - Waterloo	192.75
19-4-66	1835 Bournemouth Cen - Waterloo	300.75
23-4-66	1635 Waterloo - Southampton Cen	380.00
10-9-66	1635 Waterloo - Southampton Cen	459.25
19-9-66	11.16 Southampton Central - Waterloo	538.50
1-10-66	1755 Southampton Cen. - Waterloo	617.75
6-10-66	1709 Waterloo - Basingstoke	665.50
10-12-66	1442 Bournemouth Cen - Waterloo	773.50
24-12-66	1514 Southampton Cen - Waterloo	852.75
28-12-66	1314 Basingstoke - Waterloo	900.50
29-12-66	1709 Waterloo - Basingstoke	948.25
7-1-67	1914 Southampton Cen - Waterloo	1,027.50
18-1-67	1330 Waterloo - Southampton Cen.	1,116.75
8-3-67	1635 Waterloo - Southampton Cen.	1,196.00
23-3-67	1520 Waterloo - Bournemouth CH.	1,304.00
WITHDRAWN 26 MAR 1967		1,304.00

north', because the distances were smaller on the SR – with less choice of services – more careful planning was required. Travelling from London, the furthest west you could go, without being stranded for the night, was Brockenhurst on the 21.20 from Waterloo where, after a wait of 39 minutes (23.35 to 00.14), a connection into the 22.13 Up Mails Weymouth to Waterloo was made.

Boarding at Brockenhurst, and if right-time running was enjoyed, nearly three hours' sleep could be enjoyed. With long station stops while GPO and railway staff set about their duties, it was only the creaking and sighing of the suspension that indicated we were once more on our way. Securely ensconced in a warm compartment it was a world away from the conditions of present-day rail travel – glaring fluorescent lighting, continuous announcements, IPods and phones, none of which are conducive to getting one's head down. Rather than being stranded at Waterloo in the early hours you could, by alighting at Woking for a 29-minute connection, transfer into the 02.45 Papers Waterloo to Bournemouth (03.00 to 03.29). This plan was sometimes at risk when, after dieselisation of the Up Mail, the diesel was failed and a substitute steam provided – not always immediately – the late running meaning a curtailed longer fester in the often cold, early hours at Basingstoke was endured. I was to travel on the Up Mails (officially diagrammed a Class 47 diesel in later months) a total of fifteen times and was fortunate to travel on the last steam-operated Mails in both directions.

Chasing explained

An activity often referred to within this book is chasing – a pursuit certain individuals among the regular travelling group I was associated with during those halcyon days often undertook. The objective was to attain over 1,000 miles behind as many different Pacifics as possible and, with the end nigh, we competed with each other in a sort of healthy rivalry to be the first between ourselves to do just that. Often thwarted by withdrawals or failures it was very much hit and miss – but it all added to the camaraderie and competitive nature of our hobby. Chasing 'Merchant 8' *Orient Line* for mileage one Wednesday in September 1966, I travelled with her on the 15.30 Waterloo to Weymouth and back on the 22.13 Up Mails – which she worked throughout. On Friday of the same week she worked the 17.30 from Waterloo to Bournemouth from which I alighted at Southampton. Returning to Basingstoke with No. 34036 *Westward Ho!* before catching the 21.20 ex-Waterloo with No. 34009 *Lyme Regis*, I was very surprised when *Orient Line* turned up at Brockenhurst on the Up Mails – the train obviously having been re-engined at Bournemouth. The motive power foremen at the remaining steam depots often worked miracles to keep the service running and had to make use of what ever

Opposite, top: My unofficial log of the progress of the 22.13 Weymouth to Waterloo (Up Mail) on the 23/24 September 1966 behind Unmodified Pacific No. 34102 *Lapford*.

Opposite, bottom: An example (in this case with 'Merchants' Nos 35013/4) of the type of documentation we like-minded individuals compiled during the increasingly long waits between steam services.

was available to them rather than sticking rigidly to the 'booked' diagrams. The total number of locomotives I obtained over 1,000 miles with was fifteen with two (35007 and 35023) over 2,000. Some days were good and some were bad. Obviously, as time went by, the catches became fewer and I reasoned with myself that the ever-accumulating steam mileage was history being made – and one day it would all be gone!

Dieselisation

With the diesel-minded Western Region having taken over the routes west of Salisbury during 1963 it was only a matter of time before the West of England services out of Waterloo were affected. Come September 1964 and all the through-services, including the prestigious 'Atlantic Coast Express', were truncated at Exeter and dieselised. Those steam locomotives unfortunate enough to be allocated at Exmouth Junction (Exeter) and throughout Devon faced mass withdrawal – with just a few, presumably the most recently overhauled, escaping elsewhere within the remaining SR steam sheds. The two-hourly Waterloo to Exeter service was taken over by 'Warship' diesels (latterly Class 42) but there were many occasions whereby Salisbury shed came to the rescue with whatever was available. Rarely working west of Salisbury, numerous instances were noted by myself with No. 34018 *Axminster* working out of Waterloo on the 10.00 service on 16 June 1967 perhaps being the final substitution? A somewhat mystifying locomotive diagramming scenario was programmed from 28 November 1966 to 2 January 1967 with the 19.00 Waterloo to Exeter being booked steam to Salisbury where the 'Warship' from the preceding 17.41 commuter train ex-Waterloo took over. On 6 December 1966, however, the 'Warship' ran out of fuel prior to working the 17.41 and No. 34019 *Bideford* stepped in. The following day the 'Warship' failed on the inward leg with *Bideford* coming to the rescue again!

The other dieselisation came in October 1966 when SR were allocated six Brush 4s (Class 47) to 'assist' timekeeping problems being encountered in connection with the deteriorating condition of the remaining steam fleet. To compile a list of all the services they failed to operate would lead to one of some considerable length – perhaps indicating their (un)reliability one day (14 December 1966) NONE of the six were working. The sudden short-notice replacement which frequently occurred must have been the running foreman's nightmare i.e. providing not only a fit locomotive but two men as opposed to one – but to us enthusiasts it was sheer joy. Although never proved, I am sure that rumours of sabotage involving bags of sugar and loose fuel caps/covers had some foundation! Having by default travelled with all six at one time or another I was surprised when, on 10 July 1967, the SR management did not send them back to wherever they came from immediately – keeping them for a further year perhaps as a future surety for failures. The most prominent delay I witnessed was on 3 May 1967 when D1925 failed at Woking while working the 05.30 Waterloo to Bournemouth service. Guildford shed eventually sent up Standard 3MT No. 76069, which took the Class 1 service forward some two hours late. The prestigious 'Bournemouth Belle' was often, during the last few months, worked by a dirty unkempt short-notice steam replacement – a contrast to the brown and cream vehicles, which were always kept in pristine condition.

Deputising for a diesel failure on the 12.30 'Bournemouth Belle' departure on 12 March 1967 was Weymouth's 'Merchant Navy' No. 35028 *Clan Line*. I paid the supplement and travelled with her on that day together with seven further occasions (accumulating 1,727 miles) before her withdrawal at Nine Elms that July – and heading off into preservation.

No. 196770
BRITISH RAILWAYS BOARD
PULLMAN SERVICES
PASSENGER'S CHECK   Good for this Trip only when accompanied by an appropriate Railway Ticket

PASSENGERS ARE EARNESTLY REQUESTED TO SEE THAT TICKETS ARE TORN FROM A BOOK, CORRECTLY FILLED IN, SIGNED AND DATED, AND TO DESTROY THE TICKET AT THE END OF THE JOURNEY

Car...One Seat
From.......................................to.....................
....19.......
4/-   ....CONDUCTOR
SEE CONDITIONS AT BACK

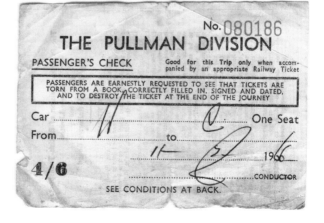

No. 080186
THE PULLMAN DIVISION
PASSENGER'S CHECK   Good for this Trip only when accompanied by an appropriate Railway Ticket

PASSENGERS ARE EARNESTLY REQUESTED TO SEE THAT TICKETS ARE TORN FROM A BOOK, CORRECTLY FILLED IN, SIGNED AND DATED, AND TO DESTROY THE TICKET AT THE END OF THE JOURNEY

Car ....One Seat
From.......................................to.....................
..................................19 66....
4/6   ....CONDUCTOR
SEE CONDITIONS AT BACK

The price of luxury – excess on my season ticket!

The dwindling numbers

With Redhill closing to steam the previous summer there were, by January 1966, just 226 steam locomotives allocated to the SR's seven remaining sheds. They were 70A (Nine Elms), 70B (Feltham), 70C (Guildford), 70D (Eastleigh), 70E (Salisbury), 70F (Bournemouth) and 70G (Weymouth) all of which, with the exception of Feltham, fortunately had passenger work allocated to them. Although often visiting other parts of the country whenever lines were closing or 'last occasions' were enacted, i.e. steam services being dieselised or the last surviving members of a particular class being withdrawn, it became my increasing obsessional trait to catch all of my home territory's allocation before it was too late. Whenever a general overhaul was due or an 'expensive' failure occurred the locomotive concerned was, taking into account the associated costs, condemned. This of course reduced my 'needs' list had I have not achieved a run behind her, but made the chase ever more urgent for those that remained. Although initially thirteen classes saw in New Year's Day in January 1966, on main line services just over a year later a mere eight (totalling 122) had survived. I detail below a brief résumé of the characteristics of those final eight classes and (in date order) my final catches of them. The 'Jan 1966–SR allocation' and 'Preservation' headings denote the number of locomotives in the January 1966 SR allocation and the number in preservation.

Type	Number Series	Built
BR Standard 5MT	73000–171	1951–7
Tractive effort	Weight (excluding tender)	Driving wheel
26,120	76 tons	6ft 2in
Jan 1966 –SR allocation	Preservation	Designer
31	5	Riddles

Built at Derby and Doncaster, these versatile 4–6–0 mixed traffic locomotives were allocated mainly to the LMS and Scottish regions with just twenty being initially assigned to the SR. These worked the Kent coast and Bournemouth semi-fast services and received names from the 'King Arthur' locomotives they replaced. Proving an adequate substitution for the worn-out ex-SR stock an eventual total of forty-five, the balance having been displaced from elsewhere in Britain, saw service on the SR.

Saturday 28 May 1966 – No. 73002 on the 13.52 Bournemouth Central to Eastleigh
A day trip out of Waterloo to Hampshire started behind 'Merchant Navy' No. 35026 *Lamport & Holt Line* on the 09.30 semi-fast for Bournemouth. Having doubled back from Southampton to Eastleigh with Banbury's No. 44780 on the Poole to York Inter-Regional service, I returned to Southampton in order to bash some local services for some of either Eastleigh or Bournemouth-allocated lower-powered classes not seen on Waterloo services. Bored with nothing around, I visited Lymington with tank No. 80085 – just for something different! The connecting stopping service back to Southampton at Brockenhurst had Weymouth-allocated No. 73002 working it – what luck! Although she was to last until March the following year I was never to ride with her again.

Type	Number Series	Built
SR WC/BoB 7P6F	34001–110	1945–51
Tractive effort	**Weight (excluding tender)**	**Driving wheel**
27,715	86/90 tons	6ft 2in
Jan 1966–SR allocation	**Preservation**	**Designer**
54	20	Bulleid

Built at Brighton and Eastleigh these 110 4–6–2 Pacifics were designed as a lighter version of the 'Merchant Navy' class – and as such could work services on all routes throughout the SR. Initially used on Kent coast expresses, upon electrification they migrated to the South Western Division. Differentiated merely by name, sixty of the 'West Country' (named after destinations served by the SR) and 'Battle of Britain' (names with wartime connections – mainly RAF squadrons) locomotives were modified (air-smoothed casing removed) during their lives. Those which retained the casing became affectionately known as 'spam cans'. The prime minister Winston Churchill's funeral train, locomotive No. 34051 *Winston Churchill*, is preserved as a static exhibit at the National Railway Museum, York.

Tuesday 31 May 1966 – No. 34002 Salisbury on the 17.00 Waterloo to Exeter St Davids

While on my usual evening commute out of Waterloo I was wandering along platform 10 to see No. 34086 *219 Squadron* at the head of the 17.09 departure when there was a station announcement to the effect that the 17.00 Exeter service was to depart from platform 14. Not taking much notice upon reaching the front of the 17.09 I could see an engine furiously blowing off from the vicinity of platform 14 so just out of interest I climbed into the 17.09 stock crossing over and looking out – steam was on the normally diesel-operated Exeter service! I looked at my watch. It showed 16.58½. I jumped out, rushed back up the platform, down the subway, along it, up the stairs and into the train with seconds to spare! I am sure that this sort of activity has enabled me, over the years, to avoid obesity. Initially boarding the train for the novelty value of a trip of 66½ miles to Andover, it wasn't until the first stop, at Woking, that I was to ascertain that working it was No. 34002 *Salisbury* – my last required Pacific! She came off the train at Salisbury (the WR not permitting steam any further) and worked the following day's 18.38 back to Waterloo – which I caught from Basingstoke!

Type	Number Series	Built
SR MN 8P	35001–30	1941–9
Tractive effort	**Weight (excluding tender)**	**Driving wheel**
33,495	97 tons	6ft 2in
Jan 1966 – SR allocation	**Preservation**	**Designer**
16	10	Bulleid

Thirty of these magnificent 4–6–2 machines were built at Eastleigh. The most powerful locomotive ever built for the SR they were, resulting from their weight, restricted to the region's main lines. Some were used on Continental boat services to the Kent ports before joining their sisters on the south-western main line expresses to Bournemouth and Exeter. All were modified (air-smoothed casing removed) during their lives and were named after famous shipping lines thus giving them the nickname of 'Packets'. No. 35029 *Ellerman Lines* is a sectioned exhibit at the National Railway Museum, York.

Wednesday 1 June 1966 – No. 35012 United States Lines on the 17.30 Waterloo to Bournemouth Central
Caught while on a 'normal' evenings commute, I was to eventually accumulate over 1,300 miles with her before her demise just ten months hence.

Type	Number Series	Built
BR Standard 4MT	75000–79	1951–7
Tractive effort	**Weight (excluding tender)**	**Driving wheel**
25,515	69 tons	5ft 8in
Jan 1966 – SR allocation	**Preservation**	**Designer**
11	3	Riddles

Eighty of these lighter versions of the Standard 4–6–0s were built at Swindon and distributed between the LMS, Western and Southern regions. The SR allocation (fifteen) were, in 1957, equipped with large tenders and fitted with double chimneys to improve efficiency.

Saturday 1 October 1966 – No. 75075 on the 04.40 Waterloo to Salisbury
Although used on stopping and semi-fast services, being fewer in number and inferior to Bulleids and Standard 5s, they were often the foreman's last resort – and subsequently difficult to catch. Having missed two through withdrawals I consider myself fortunate in catching the ones that I did. Having been chasing 'Merchant Navy' No. 35008 *Orient Line* for mileage during the previous few days I had just arrived with her into Waterloo at 03.48 on the Up Mails. I wasn't bothered what was working the 04.40 stopper for Salisbury, it was just a train I could put my head down upon – but it was my last 75xxx! The day got even better with two 80xxx Tanks on New Forest stopping services and, would you believe, another 93 miles with *Orient Line*.

Type	Number Series	Built
BR Standard 3MT	82000–44	1952–5
Tractive effort	**Weight**	**Driving wheel**
21,490	73 tons	5ft 3in
Jan 1966 – SR allocation	**Preservation**	**Designer**
9	0	Riddles

All of these 2–6–2T tank locomotives were built at Swindon for usage on branch lines and secondary passenger services principally on the Southern and Western regions. A new-build (82045) is at present under construction.

Friday 30 December 1966 – No. 82029 on the 08.16 Clapham Junction to Kensington Olympia

Many of these tank locomotives had migrated to Nine Elms from various parts of the SR and WR as areas had become dieselised or branch lines that they were employed upon had closed. The main purpose of Nine Elms' tank allocation was to work the many ECS moves between Clapham Yard and Waterloo together with the area's shunting requirements. By 1966 'The Kenny Belle' (detailed in chapter 17) was the ONLY passenger trains they worked and No. 82029 was the fourth 70A 82xxx that was caught while working it.

Type	Number Series	Built
BR Standard 4MT	80000–154	1951–7
Tractive effort	Weight	Driving wheel
25,515	88 tons	5ft 8in
Jan 1966 – SR allocation	Preservation	Designer
33	15	Riddles

155 of these well-liked versatile 2–6–4T tanks were built at Brighton, Derby and Doncaster. A further fifteen were cancelled in the light of impending dieselisation brought forward by the 1955 modernisation plan. Designed for suburban and semi-fast passenger work they were probably best known for the sterling work on the LT&S lines out of Fenchurch Street. Initially allocated to all regions except the Western, the SR members were to found working throughout Kent and East Sussex – before migrating to the South Western Division.

Friday 7 April 1967 – No. 80139 on the 17.20 Eastleigh to Fratton

I caught over thirty of these handsome Brighton-designed locomotives – mainly on the SR. All but this one had been caught during 1964, '65 and '66 but, because Eastleigh never seemed to turn her out for any other passenger services other than the 17.20 SX Eastleigh to Fratton (operated principally for Eastleigh Works employees), I had to take a valuable half-day annual leave in the hope that she, on that day, would stay on the same duty. She did – and I got her.

Type	Number Series	Built
LMS 2MT	41200–329	1946–52
Tractive effort	Weight	Driving wheel
17,410/18,510	63 tons	5ft 0in
January 1966 –SR allocation	Preservation	Designer
13	4	Ivatt

Ex-Redhill, now Eastleigh-allocated BR Standard 2–6–4T No. 80139 *never* seemed to work anything other than the 17.20 SX Eastleigh to Fratton workers' train. On 7 April 1967 I took a valuable half-day's leave and caught a run with her (my final required 80xxx in the country) – seen here at Fareham.

Built at Crewe and Derby the first 100 of these 2–6–2T tank locomotives were allocated to the LMS – the remainder to the SR. Used throughout the SR on branch line passenger work with the continual reduction of requirements, their last stronghold was Nine Elms.

Monday 22 May 1967 – No. 41319 on the 08.16 Clapham Junction to Kensington Olympia

The only 'Mickey' Tank I wanted in the whole country. For at least two years Eastleigh's only member of that class was seemingly permanently allocated as the East Yard pilot – always tantalisingly being sighted when passing by. Eastleigh had no passenger duties for her but because Nine Elms became short of power following many withdrawals of the aforementioned 82xxx class, she was transferred there. It was only a matter of time, at least that was what I hoped, before she turned up on 'The Kenny Belle' – and I was there. She also had the dubious honour of working the last morning's services on Friday 7 July.

Type	Number Series	Built
BR Standard 4MT	76000–114	1952–7
Tractive effort	**Weight (excluding tender)**	**Driving wheel**
24,170	59 tons	5ft 3in
Jan 1966 – SR allocation	**Preservation**	**Designer**
26	4	Riddles

115 of these lighter versions of the 4MT 75xxx series were built at Horwich and Doncaster. They were allocated to all regions except the Western for use on cross-country passenger and freight services – the latter particularly useful in view of the weight-restricted sidings often used. The SR's initial allocation, at Eastleigh and Bournemouth, of thirty-seven swelled over the years as displaced members from elsewhere within Britain migrated southwards.

Monday 26 June 1967 – No. 76007 on the 16.46 Weymouth to Woking

I left this one a bit late – only two weeks to go before steam's cessation on the SR. Having monitored her on the office power log (a human forerunner of automated reporting) the ONLY passenger service I was liable to catch her on was the above stopping service. For weeks she had only worked freight and parcel trains, UNTIL that night. As it was a Monday – i.e. a late duty in the office – I could only make it from Micheldever – for just the 10¼ miles between there and Basingstoke. Still, she was the LAST SR locomotive I required so I had to make the effort!

Only like-minded enthusiasts can appreciate the resultant sense of achievement upon subsequently scoring through the relevant entries in their ever-present Ian Allan ABC publication – thus completing each individual section. So, the reader may ask, how did I fare in the chase? Of the main line classes of Standard 5s, 'Merchant Navy's and Light Pacifics I missed only one, No. 34041 *Wilton*, she being withdrawn in January 1966 but could have been out of use some months previously. With no booked passenger work I was unlikely to catch the Guildford-allocated Moguls Nos 31408, 31803, 76012 and 76059 as with Weymouth's No. 41301. I didn't start commuting via 'The Kenny Belle' until the November of 1966 thus missing Nine Elms-allocated Nos 80069, 80095, 82006, 82018, 82024, 82026 and 82028 tanks, I even discovered, when sorting out all my long lost negatives for processing via John Bird's Southern Images website, one was of No. 82018 storming away on the Kensington train – without me aboard! Eastleigh's Nos 75065, 75066, 76019, 76063, 80065, 80082 and 80142, Bournemouth's Nos 41316, 76010, 76057, 80013 and Ryde's W16, W22, W31 and W5 tanks were, how can I put it, just missed. The end result was that I managed runs behind 84 per cent of the steam stock, as at 1 January 1966 – you can't win them all!

12

THE ISLAND REVISITED

I returned to the Isle of Wight again in September 1965 when, similar to my visit the previous year, the weather was hot and sunny crossing the Solent, once again courtesy of MV *Southsea*, a ship that saw forty years' service under BR and then Sealink ownership. The 'voyage' itself (often used by myself nowadays, albeit by car ferries to Fishbourne), still gives the impression that you are leaving the country and puts you in the holiday spirit even before arriving on this idyllic island. W28 *Ashey* was in charge of the 11.18 Cowes departure and with doors slammed shut (remember them?), the departure was a slickly organised a mere eight minutes after the boat's arrival. Having obtained a lineside permit, which allows photography from railway property away from the normal station environment, I was able to photograph (albeit not entirely successfully) the trains from positions such as above the entrance to the tunnel at Wroxall (through which trains to Ventnor had to travel) and the steam shed at Ryde – without today's health and safety measures such as the fluorescent high visibility vests!

Ventnor station was surrounded by sheer cliffs drawing immediate comparisons with a Roman amphitheatre and perhaps was the most photogenic of all the picture postcard stations and termini. Seemingly precariously situated on a ledge carved out of St Boniface Down, 294ft above sea level and high above the town, Ventnor station was always going to be at the mercy of the 1,312-yard long tunnel's condition; its upkeep doubtless contributed to the running costs and, in the following April, the line's closure – although today's use of it as an important water supply would perhaps cast doubts on its alleged condition back then. Ventnor's claim to fame is that, being both south-facing and in a sheltered position, the temperate air not only attracted Victorians sent by their doctors for remedial medicinal purposes but allowed various Mediterranean-type plants to grow there as can be seen in the town's Botanic Gardens. With the threatened closure of the Smallbrook Junction–Cowes and Shanklin–Ventnor sections, I once again covered the entire system. Five hours after arrival on the island, and three catches later, I returned to Ryde and paid a visit to the shed where I was able to wander at will photographing these locomotives in various stages of repair or abandonment. Several coaches had been recently repainted with, internally, cream ceilings, fawn luggage racks and seating recovered with BR upholstery. Together with a fresh green paint coating externally, it gave one the effect of being on a museum exhibit – not part of a working railway. One can only regret the potential of the island's

SATURDAYS, 19th JUNE to 4th SEPTEMBER, 1965 and 4th JUNE to 3rd SEPTEMBER, 1966

C14	**SATURDAYS**	Cowes, Newport, Ventnor, Sandown and Ryde

UP (first section)

Station		ECS	ECS		ECS	ECS		LE	LE			LE
COWES	dep 1			05†10							06 39	
Mill Hill	2										06 41½	
Gas Works Siding	3											
Medina Wharf	4											
NEWPORT	arr 5			05†20							06 50	
	dep 6										06 52	
Havenstreet	arr 7										07 03	
	dep 8										07 08	
Ashey	9											
VENTNOR	dep 10						06 35					
Wroxall	arr 11						06 40					
	dep 12						06 41					
Shanklin	arr 13						06 47					
	dep 14						06 48					
Sandown	arr 15						06 52					
	dep 16						06 54					09 4?
Brading	arr 17						06 58					09 5
	dep 18						06 59					09 5
Smallbrook Jn.	19						07 04			07 11½		
RYDE St. John's Road	20	03†12	03†20		06†15		06‖50 06‖55 07a07		07b15			07‖35
„ Esplanade	21						07a11		07c20			
„ PIER HEAD	arr 22	03†17	03†25		06†20		06‖55 07‖00 07 13		07 22			07‖40 10 0?
RYDE PIER Boat	23			04 50			06 50				07 30	
PORTSMOUTH Hbr.	24			05 20			07 20				08 00	

UP (second section)

Station			LE								ECS		
COWES	dep 1	09 28					10 28					
Mill Hill	2	09 30½					10 30½					
Gas Works Siding	3											
Medina Wharf	4											
NEWPORT	arr 5	09 39					10 39					
	dep 6	09 42½					10 42½		11†05			
Havenstreet	arr 7	09 52					10X52					
	dep 8	09 55					10 55		11 15			
Ashey	9	10 00					11 00					
VENTNOR	dep 10		09 40				10 20		10 40			
Wroxall	arr 11		09X45				10 25		10X45			
	dep 12		09 46				10 26		10 46			
Shanklin	arr 13		09X52				10X32		10X52			
	dep 14		09 57	10 12			10 37		10 55		11 12	
Sandown	arr 15		10 01						10 59			
	dep 16		10 03		10 16	10 31 10 41			11 01		11 16	
Brading	arr 17		10 07		10 20	10 35			11 05		11 20	
	dep 18		10 08		10 23	10 39			11 08		11 23	
Smallbrook Jn.	19	10 04	10 13	10 28		10 44 10 50½ 11 04			11 13	11 23	11 28	
RYDE St. John's Road	20	10c08	10a16	10‖23		11c08			11a16	11†25		
„ Esplanade	21	10c13	10c21			11c13			11c21			
„ PIER HEAD	arr 22	10 15	10 23	10‖28 10 35		10 50 10 57 11 15			11 23		11 35	
RYDE PIER Boat	23		10 20			10 50		11 20				11 50
PORTSMOUTH Hbr.	24		10 50		11 20	11 50						12 20

UP (third section)

Station			LE					LE				LE
COWES	dep 1	13 28					14 28				
Mill Hill	2	13 30½					14 30½				
Gas Works Siding	3										
Medina Wharf	4										
NEWPORT	arr 5	13 39					14 39				
	dep 6	13 42½					14 42½				
Havenstreet	arr 7	13X52					14X52				
	dep 8	13 55					14 55				
Ashey	9	14 00					15 00				
VENTNOR	dep 10	13 20	13 40				14 20		14 40		
Wroxall	arr 11	13X25	13X45				14X25		14X45		
	dep 12	13 26	13 46				14 26		14 46		
Shanklin	arr 13	13X32	13X52				14X32		14X52		
	dep 14	13 35	13 55	14 12			14 35		14 55		
Sandown	arr 15	13 39	13 59				14 39		14 59		
	dep 16	13 42	14 01		14 16	14 31	14 42		15 01		
Brading	arr 17		14 05		14 20	14 35			15 05		
	dep 18		14 08		14 23	14 39			15 08		
Smallbrook Jn.	19	13 50½ 14 04	14 13	14 28		14 44 14 50½ 15 04			15 13	15‖23
RYDE St. John's Road	20	13b54 14c08	14a16 14‖23	14‖40		14b54 15c08		15a16	15‖23
„ Esplanade	21	13c59 14c13	14c21	14‖45		14c59 15c13		15c21	
„ PIER HEAD	arr 22	14 01 14 15	14 23 14‖28 14 35		14 50 15 01 15 15			15 23	15‖28
RYDE PIER Boat	23	14 20				14 50		15 20		
PORTSMOUTH Hbr.	24	14 50				15 20		15 50		

An extract from the summer 1965 Isle of Wight working timetable.

Looking a little worse for wear was W28 *Ashey* at Ryde Pier Head on 21 September 1965 awaiting the guards right away with the 11.18 departure for Cowes.

W29 *Alverstone* departs Brading on 21 September 1965 with the 11.37 freight Shanklin to Ryde St Johns Road – as with all locomotives on the island bunker first into Ryde.

A view of W27 *Merstone* from the footbridge at Newport on 21 September 1965 preparing to work the 17.05 SX 'rush hour extra' for Ryde St Johns Road. Once the junction for four different routes, no trace of the site now exists – the nearby section of the island's only dual carriageway catering for today's commuters.

Earlier that day W28 *Ashey* was captured departing Ryde St Johns Road with a schools ECS for Shanklin. She was one of eight withdrawn at the cessation of passenger services operated by steam in December 1966 – two (W24 and W31) being kept until March 1967 for engineering trains in connection with the electrification.

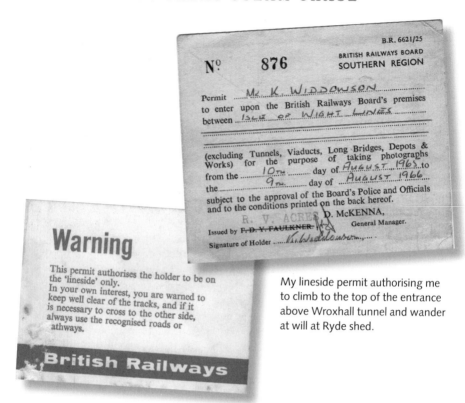

My lineside permit authorising me to climb to the top of the entrance above Wroxhall tunnel and wander at will at Ryde shed.

railway as a tourist attraction was not apparent and acted upon before it was too late. If only an entrepreneurial individual (with cash!) such as Richard Branson or Pete Waterman had been around at the time – what a mecca for tourism it would have become. Perhaps even the unique Ryde Pier Head tramway, provided to move the masses from ship to shore and closed in 1969, would have survived.

Catching the 16.25 to Newport I alighted there and visited the town for something to eat before making one last return trip to Cowes courtesy of W26 *Whitwell*. The MV *Southsea* was waiting at Ryde Pier Head with the 19.30 sailing and an unremarkable journey home saw me arrive there at 23.00 hours – the completion of a wonderful fifteen-hour day at a cost of 16s 2d.

One final visit was made in December 1966 – the last month of steam operation. With fellow enthusiast 'the Squire' from Aylesbury, a dapper and somewhat eccentric character who was always smartly dressed with bow-tie and flamboyant sports jacket, we travelled overnight into Portsmouth on the 02.30 Papers from Waterloo, courtesy of Unmodified 'West Country' No. 34102 *Lapford* (unkindly nicknamed *Clapford* on account of unusually loud persistent clanking noise emanating from her motion), and it was still pitch black as MV *Southsea* (again!) readied herself for her 06.40 departure – possibly the emptiest crossing I have ever made of the Solent. With all the steam services now only operating between Ryde Esplanade and Shanklin, we had to catch one of the petrol-powered tramcars between the Pier Head and Esplanade stations before boarding the 07.30

departure with W28 *Ashey*. I caught four of the five locomotives in circulation that day – hunger necessitating visiting the seafront at Shanklin for breakfast, hence missing the fifth. Mission completed, I returned to Portsmouth on the 11.30 sailing, travelling over to Southampton for further steam haulage on the SR main line.

The remaining 'stub' between Ryde and the two popular east coast resorts of Sandown and Shanklin was to be closed at the end of the year for three months' work in preparation for electrification utilising recently displaced 1938 ex-London Underground stock which, during the 1990s, were embellished with vinyl dinosaur logos highlighting the island's fossil finds over the years. I have returned many times to this wonderful island – on one occasion even hiring bikes with my daughter to ride along some of the many closed railways on the island which have been converted to a network of cycle paths – but will never forget those superb days when it seemed the clock was turned back and for a few cherished hours the fast pace of modern-day living was forgotten. The film *The Railway Children* (although filmed elsewhere), depicting the slower pace of life with folk turning and waving at the three-coach steam train passing through such a Sylvan setting, is how I remember the railways of the island. A visit to the preserved line between Smallbrook Junction and Wootton is a must as it authentically replicates the Edwardian railway scene encountered by travellers prior to steam's cessation in 1966.

13

SABOTAGED &
DEFEATED

The title of this chapter is perhaps an unjust soubriquet for the railway line which ran between the Bristol Channel and the South Coast, originally known as the Somerset & Dorset Joint Railway. Alternatives to the S&D, as I will now refer to it, were 'Slow & Dirty' or 'Serene & Delightful', depending on how the traveller saw it. A complicated history of the piecemeal opening of various sections of the route over the Mendips and along the Stour Valley, is best left to those more knowledgeable than I. All I will say that is the 'missing link', i.e.

At 05.15 hours on a July 1965 morning I visited Templecombe (83G) shed. Wandering around (unchallenged) an air of neglect and abandonment seemed to prevail – the silent locomotives dripping with early morning mist. This photograph depicts a line of locomotives already condemned and awaiting removal to the breakers – Nos 9647, 9670, 41214, 80067, 41243 and 41296.

that between Templecombe and Blandford Forum, was completed in 1863 and through-services between the Bristol Channel port of Highbridge and Hampshire began from that date. The 'spur' over the Mendips from Evercreech to Bath was completed eleven years later and became the main line, relegating the original route over the Somerset Levels via Glastonbury to that of a feeder branch. Hopes to cream off lucrative sea-borne freight, which had to travel around Land's End, while successful did not realise the intended potential and the route settled down to serve the requirements of predominantly intermediate passenger traffic and coal from Somerset.

Summer Saturdays, however, was when the line came into prominence. When this route through the Mendips and Stour Valley had Inter-Regional traffic from all over Britain it must have been fascinating to travel over or observe, with the lengthy trains requiring a second locomotive, often freight representatives from classes such as ex-S&D 8F 2–8–0s or BR Standard 9F 2–10–0s being used, over the gradient-strewn northern section. The success of the Inter-Regional trains was basically down to years of commendable advertising by the LMS who highlighted the benefits of not changing trains when travelling from home to holiday. The whole system appeared to be in a time warp with no attempt at modernisation with improved (in the form of diesel) services or investment in the infrastructure. The footfall had declined during the late 1950s, a double whammy effect caused by post-war affluence and the associated increased car ownership, and the few express services that remained, including 'The Pines Express' (so named from the topography associated with Bournemouth's trees), by 1962 had been deliberately diverted over more circuitous routes. This was to ensure that when Beeching's accountants reviewed the financial case for retention the inevitable decision was arrived at. Similar to the former Great Central route into Marylebone, the stock, infrastructure, and locomotives were left to gradually deteriorate. By the time of my first visit in 1964 there was the noticeable atmosphere of abandonment and neglect usually associated during the 1960s as a precursor to closure.

By 1965, after dieselisation of the Exeter services, the 'steamiest' route – i.e. the one which avoided diesel services as far as possible, an increasingly difficult task – from London to the S&D was by using the 22.35 mails from Waterloo to Eastleigh then across via Salisbury to either Templecombe or Bristol. In July of that year I chose the former and having arrived at Templecombe at 05.00, and with nothing moving on the line until over two hours later, a visit to the engine shed was made. With ten locomotives simmering quietly and seven dead, an eerie silence with an overall atmosphere of neglect saturated the mist-filled dawn. This scenario was never going to last forever and although grateful that I witnessed part of history being acted out, it was an emotional roller-coaster of thoughts every time 'last' visits were made anywhere. The only Templecombe-allocated engine not at her home shed that morning was BR 4MT No. 75073 – subsequently being seen on the first northbound train (07.10 ex-Bournemouth West) crossed en route while heading south with sister locomotive No. 75072. Returning two months later, this time via Bristol where the same scenario occurred (i.e. arrival in the early hours and to having time to kill while waiting for the S&D services to commence running) on this occasion a return diesel unit-operated branch line service to Severn Beach was undertaken. I was indeed fortunate that day because out of the three departures that morning from Bristol Temple Meads to Bath Green Park (06.00, 07.50 and 09.00) only the 07.50 departure, with me luckily aboard, was steam-worked

BR 3MT 2–6–2T No. 82041 appears dwarfed within the fading grandeur of the ex-Midland Railways Bath Green Park terminus on 18 September 1965 with the 10.10 departure for Bristol Temple Meads. Fortunately saved for the people of Bath after its closure six months later, it is now used as an indoor market and events space.

BR Standard 4MT No. 80039 leads the 09.00 Bristol Temple Meads to Branksome (with No. 73068 as the train locomotive) down the incline between Templecombe Upper and Lower stations on 18 September 1965. No doubt auditors accessing the line's finances frowned upon this seemingly costly method used when the S&D trains were required to call at the main line station.

(No. 82041) the others being Hymek diesels. After bashing the shed at Bath Green Park I waited at the now-preserved station for the four-vehicle 09.00 Bristol to Bournemouth train which upon reversal was re-engined with BR Standard 5MT No. 73068 which was to take me over the 37 miles to Templecombe.

   What a splendidly engineered line this was. Immediately upon departure from Bath there was an awesome 2-mile 1 in 50 climb, providing panoramic views of the city, to the tunnel at Combe Down. This was Britain's longest unventilated tunnel (1,829 yards) through which I believe the crew had to cover their faces with wet cloths to avoid asphyxiation. Then, after a short run down into Midford, 8 more miles of 1 in 50/60 was encountered to the summit at Masbury (811ft). As if that wasn't enough, there was then 7 miles of downhill switchback to Evercreech through splendidly unspoilt countryside – the described scenario so adequately encapsulated by the well-known railway photographer Ivo Peters. I feel sorry for those who never had the opportunity to appreciate this enchanting Somerset vista from the luxury of a railway carriage. The countryside I travelled through that day is naturally still there for present-day car owners but viewing it while leaning out of the carriage window getting smothered in cinders and deafened by exhaust echoing off the frequent rock faces and deep cuttings is surely not the same. I returned to London that day via the Highbridge branch on the 13.15 from Evercreech Junction. The ex-GWR power provided eighteen months previously had given way to a relatively modern Ivatt Tank (No. 41223) which, in comparison to my journey from Bath earlier that day, was somewhat extreme in that it was just one tank engine hauling one coach and one van which hardly required any effort over the Somerset Levels! With connections off of the S&D services not necessarily customer-led, I festered at a deserted Highbridge for an hour before eventually proceeding via Bridgwater to Bristol behind the inevitable diesel hydraulic (D7017). Homeward-bound from there to Paddington? I think not and after alighting at Chippenham at 17.48, one more track bash awaited me. It was the last day's service on the 5¼-mile diesel unit-operated branch line to Calne. For many years the passenger traffic was not the main 'income' – that was the conveyance of sausages, pies and meat products (in passenger trains) from the Calne factory of Harris & Company. Although not the last trains, the 17.56 out and 18.17 return services were well-filled with locals making their pilgrimage, so often acted out during those times on train services they were about to lose. Sustrans subsequently converted a major section of the route as part of the National Cycle Network. Yet another Western Hydraulic, D1021 *Western Cavalier*, lulled me into much-needed sleep while speeding into Paddington, depositing me there at a reasonable finishing time, for a change, of 20.36. I unusually saw my parents that evening – with homecomings normally well after their bedtime, that was indeed a novelty.

The traditional viewpoint of departing services heading north away from Evercreech Junction was utilised in taking this shot. It portrays BR 4MT 4–6–0 No. 75072 working the 11.41 Bournemouth Central to Bristol Temple Meads on 18 September 1965. The reduced service implemented the following January had no use for large locomotives such as these and she was withdrawn.

Although proposed for closure in January 1966, various problems with the substitute bus services gave the S&D a stay of execution. This also delayed the Western Region's 'ambition' of being the first region to abolish steam power – finally achieved eight weeks later in March. The appalling 'stop-gap' service was, in my opinion, deliberately designed to ward off any prospective customers – with large

REVISED SERVICE - WEEKDAYS ONLY
COMMENCING MONDAY, 3rd JANUARY, 1966

BATH GREEN PARK TO BOURNEMOUTH

							SX	SO
BATH GREEN PARK	dep.	06 45	08 15			16 25	18 10	
Midford Halt		06 57	08 27			16 37	18 22	
Wellow Halt		07 03	08 34			16 44	18 29	
Shoscombe & Single Hill Halt		07 07	08 38			16 48	18 33	
Radstock North		07 13	08 44			16 54	18 39	
Midsomer Norton South		07 20	08 51			17 01	18 47	
Chilcompton		07 28	08 59			17 09	18 55	
Binegar		07 36	09 07			17 17	19 03	
Masbury Halt		07 40	09 11			17 21	19 07	
Shepton Mallet Charlton Road		07 50	09 18			17 29	19 15	
Evercreech New		07 56	09 25			17 35	19 21	
Evercreech Junction	arr.	08 00	09 29			17 38	19 24	
Highbridge for Burnham-on-Sea	dep.	06 55			16 00			
Bason Bridge		06 59			16 05			
Edington Burtle		07 05			16 12			
Shapwick Halt		07 10			16 18			
Ashcott		07 17			16 21			
Glastonbury & Street		07 22			16 30			
West Pennard		07 31			16 42			
Pylle Halt		07 40			16 52			
Evercreech Junction	arr.	07 45			17 00			
Evercreech Junction	dep.	07 46	08 04	09 32	16 13	17 43	19 28	
Cole		—	08 13	09 38	16 20	17 48	19 34	
Wincanton		—	08 22	09 47	16 29	17 57	19 43	
TEMPLECOMBE	arr.	08 05	08 29	09 53	16 36	18 05	19 50	
	dep.	07 35		09 05	12 30	16 42		21 03	21 03
Henstridge		07 44		09 14	12 39	16 51		21 11	21 11
Stalbridge		07 51		09 19	12 47	16 55		21 16	21 15
Sturminster Newton		07 59		09 27	12 54	17 06		21 23	21 23
Shillingstone		08 06		09 37	13 00	17 12		21 29	21 29
Blandford Forum		08 17		09 47	13 10	17 22		21 39	21 39
Bailey Gate		08 28		09 59	13 21	17 33		—	21 50
Broadstone		08 40		10 20	13 32	17 50	18 32	21 58	22 04
Creekmoor Halt		08 44		10 26	13 36	17 54	18 44	22 02	22 08
Poole		08 49		10 31	13 42	18 02	18 57	22 13	22 13
Parkstone		08 56		10 38	13 47			—	—
Branksome		09 01		10 42	13 51	18 10	19 06	—	—
BOURNEMOUTH CENTRAL		09 08			13 57	18 15	19 11	22 25	22 25

REVISED SERVICE - WEEKDAYS ONLY
COMMENCING MONDAY, 3rd JANUARY, 1966

BOURNEMOUTH TO BATH GREEN PARK

								SX	SO		
BOURNEMOUTH CENTRAL	dep.	06b53	09 37	—		15 37		15 43		17 37	18 46
Branksome		07b00	09 44	13 25		15 44		15 50		17 43	18 53
Parkstone		07b05	09 48	13 29		15 48		15 53		17 47	18 57
Poole		07b10	09 53	13 34		15 54		16 00		17 55	19 05
Creekmoor Halt		07b15	09 58	13 39		16 00		16 05		18 01	19 10
Broadstone		07 32	10 02	13 44		16 05		16 09		18 05	19 14
Bailey Gate		07 42	10 12	13 54		16 15		16 19		18 15	19 24
Blandford Forum		07 52	10 25	14 05		16 26		16a30		18 27	19 34
Shillingstone		08 10	10 36	14 15		16 42				18 37	19 44
Sturminster Newton		08 16	10 42	14 21		16a49				18 43	19 50
Stalbridge		08 23	10 49	14 28						18 50	19 57
Henstridge		08 28	10 54	14 33						18 55	20 02
TEMPLECOMBE	arr.	08 37	11 03	14 42						19 04	20 11
	dep.	07 00	08 20		14 00		15 30		16 18		20 20
Wincanton		07 07	08 28		14 08		15 38		16 26		20 27
Cole		07 16	08 39		14 17		15 47		16 34		20 37
Evercreech Junction	arr.	07 23	08 44		14 23		15 53		16 39		20 43
Evercreech Junction	dep.			08 45						17 15	
Pylle Halt				V						17 19	
West Pennard				08 55						17 27	
Glastonbury & Street				09 06						17 38	
Ashcott				09 12						17 46	
Shapwick Halt				09 17						17 51	
Edington Burtle				09 22						17 57	
Bason Bridge				09 28						18 05	
Highbridge for Burnham-on-Sea	arr.			09 33						18 10	
Evercreech Junction	dep.	07 25			14 25				16 40		20 45
Evercreech New		07 31			14 31				16 46		20 51
Shepton Mallet Charlton Road		07 52			14 44				16 59		21 00
Masbury Halt									17 09		V
Binegar		08 08			14 58				17 15		
Chilcompton		08 14			15 04				17 21		
Midsomer Norton South		08 19			15 09				17 26		21 22
Radstock North		08 24			15 14				17 31		21 27
Shoscombe & Single Hill Halt		08 30			15 20				17 37		21 33
Wellow Halt		08 34			15 24				17 41		V
Midford Halt		08 40			15 30				17 47		V
BATH GREEN PARK		08 50			15 40				17 57		21 50

b — On Saturdays Bournemouth Central dep. 07 05, Branksome 07 12, Poole 07 19, Creekmoor Halt 07 24.   f — NOT Saturdays
V — Calls to set down passengers on notice being given to the guard

Above and opposite: The appalling stop-gap service offered to the public resulting from the postponed closure of January 1966. The last-minute withdrawal of replacement buses delayed the WR's ambition of becoming steam-free from that date – having had to maintain handful of locomotives until the final closure eight weeks later.

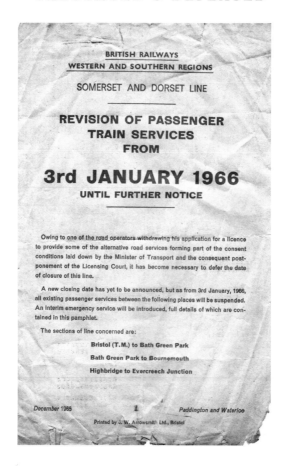

BRITISH RAILWAYS
WESTERN AND SOUTHERN REGIONS

SOMERSET AND DORSET LINE

REVISION OF PASSENGER
TRAIN SERVICES
FROM

3rd JANUARY 1966

UNTIL FURTHER NOTICE

Owing to one of the road operators withdrawing his application for a licence to provide some of the alternative road services forming part of the consent conditions laid down by the Minister of Transport and the consequent postponement of the Licensing Court, it has become necessary to defer the date of closure of this line.

A new closing date has yet to be announced, but as from 3rd January, 1966, all existing passenger services between the following places will be suspended. An interim emergency service will be introduced, full details of which are contained in this pamphlet.

The sections of line concerned are:

Bristol (T.M.) to Bath Green Park

Bath Green Park to Bournemouth

Highbridge to Evercreech Junction

December 1965   1   Paddington and Waterloo

Printed by J. W. Arrowsmith Ltd., Bristol

intervals between trains and the severing of most through-services at the midway point of Templecombe. With Bournemouth West station (the original terminating point of services from the line) having closed in September 1965, the SR were not predisposed to congest the Central station with these now non-consequential services so they were terminated at the wayside Bournemouth suburban halt of Branksome – further inconveniencing passengers. So one more visit was made and on a cold snowy February morning of 1966 (the penultimate Saturday before closure). Having for the final time travelled via Eastleigh to arrive into Bristol at 04.48, Alan (Nobby) and I found myself departing on the 06.00 Dorset-bound service with an over provision of motive power in the form of 'Warship' diesel D826 *Jupiter*. This took me to Bath where sufficient time was allowed on the through-train to once more bash the shed. With one engine in steam and six dead, this perhaps reflected the fact that a mere eight steam locomotives had been kept from the breakers yard to run the entire remaining service. Bournemouth-allocated BR 4MT No. 76011 was in charge for the remainder of the journey, taking an appalling 4 hours 31 minutes for the 82 miles from Bristol to Poole. The line has subsequently become one of the most documented in railway history and lives on in the many books and films available – nothing, however, can surpass actually having travelled the route.

The new order on the S&D after withdrawal of ex-GWR and LMS 0–6–0s the previous year came in the form of BR Standards and ex-LMS Mickey Tanks. Here, at Evercreech Junction on 18 September 1965, is Templecombe's No. 41223 preparing to shunt the one coach/van stock for the 13.15 Highbridge service into the platform.

Time arr – dep	Station	Traction	Name	Miles
22.35	Waterloo	34108	*Wincanton*	
00.45 – 02.02	Eastleigh	D7074		73½
02.27 – 03.11	Salisbury	D7047		23¾
04.48 – 06.00	Bristol Temple Meads	D826	*Jupiter*	53
	Bath Green Park	76011 *		15½
10.31 – 11.07	Poole	76013		67¾
11.18 – 11.28	Wareham	41320		7
11.40 – 11.44	Corfe Castle	80134		6
11.55 – 12.07	Wareham	34024	*Tamar Valley*	6
12.29 – 13.51	Bournemouth Central	75077		12¾
14.58 – 15.26	Southampton Central	34017	*Ilfracombe*	28¾
17.24 – 18.10	Brighton	EMU		61¼
19.21	Victoria			50¾

* assisted by No. 41290 between Templecombe Upper and Lower

ALL ABOARD THE RAILTOURS

H aving initially held the opinion that railtours were a 'cheating' way to travel behind steam locomotives, catching them working normal service trains being far more rewarding (and cheaper), I began to realise that time was running out and the only way to achieve haulage by 'rare', often freight-only locomotives was to travel on such trains and so, with the increased income generated by promotion within the clerical grades, I succumbed. Often taking convoluted circuitous routes using a plethora of different locomotives, it was on these trains that quite often friends from the Midlands and North, seen when visiting 'their' patch, were aboard and updates from the ever-changing scenario throughout Britain were exchanged. Nearly always provided with a buffet car, taking into consideration the time spent on the trains they effectively became our living quarters for the day. If overnights prior to travelling on them had been undertaken then they usually doubled as sleeping accommodation as well. I didn't travel on all the many tours run during the final eighteen months of Southern steam but here are the ones which I did:

Southampton v Wolverhampton Wanderers – Saturday 12 March 1966
No. 35027 *Port Line* – Southampton, Basingstoke, Oxford and Birmingham to Wolverhampton and return = 240 miles (I boarded and alighted at Basingstoke)

Not strictly a railtour but those aboard felt as if it was one and worth mentioning all the same. Second Division Southampton were playing away at Wolverhampton and, taking into consideration they eventually obtained promotion within weeks, had sufficient followers enough to run a 'footex' (Football excursion). Originally booked for 'Merchant Navy' No. 35028 *Clan Line*, but which had failed earlier in the week, a rather grubby No. 35027 *Port Line* was instead commandeered. Having travelled out of Waterloo on the 09.30 Bournemouth departure with No. 34034 *Honiton*, I boarded, together with six friends, the footex at Basingstoke. Poor regulation en route resulted in a thirty-four-minute late arrival at 14.20 which not only meant delaying the start of the match but also threw the non-football following contingent's plans awry.

The nearest steam services by then were those north of Shrewsbury and so catching the 14.38 Birkenhead departure (12.10 ex-Paddington) northwards with Brush Type 4 D1747 she, as expected, gave way to steam at the Shropshire town – with home-allocated Blackie No. 45311. Having inherited a by then fourteen-

This Bournemouth-allocated 'Merchant', No. 35027 *Port Line*, is seen way off her beaten track at Wolverhampton Low Level on 12 March 1966 having arrived with the 'footex' from Southampton Central. She was withdrawn that October but survives in preservation at the Bluebell Railway.

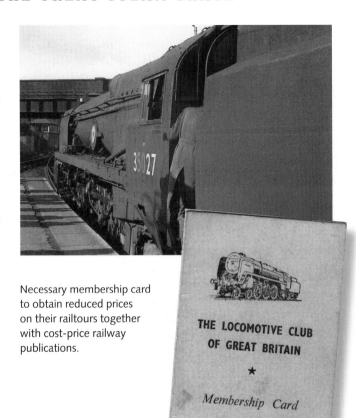

Necessary membership card to obtain reduced prices on their railtours together with cost-price railway publications.

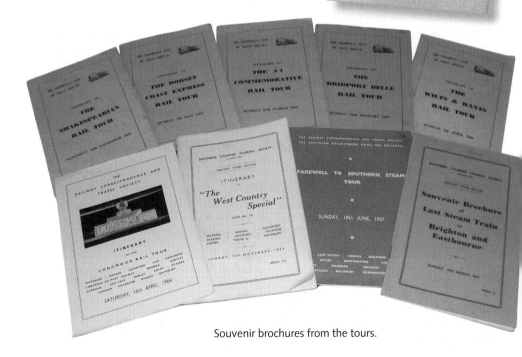

Souvenir brochures from the tours.

Souvenir tickets from the tours.

minute late running train, she was fortunate enough to manage to maintain the schedule, arriving into the first stop of Gobowen at 16.07. I said fortunate with reason because we had to change onto the 16.10 southbound service returning us to Wolverhampton to reconnect with our footex back home – or else! The road crossing gates south of the station never lifted while we raced over the footbridge to where sister No. 45277 was waiting, with the signals off, with our southbound returning service! With D1747 (again) taking over at Shrewsbury we arrived back into Wolverhampton with a mere twenty-six minutes to wait before *Port Line* took us back south. What was the score – I didn't note that fact, only entering in my notebook that word had got around among our Midland-based colleagues and the initial seven enthusiasts had swelled to twenty-six – the rarity attraction of a Southern interloper so far north warranting their attention. Arriving back into Basingstoke at 20.31 a bonus of a required Mogul, No. 76031, on the all stations stopper to Woking rounded off the day nicely.

The A4 Commemorative Rail Tour – Sunday 27 March 1966

No. 60024 *Kingfisher* – Waterloo (dep 10.05) to Exeter and return (arr 19.37) = 345 miles (via the ex-L&SWR route in both directions)

This LCGB tour utilised the visiting Aberdeen-allocated ex-LNER A4 Pacific No. 60024 *Kingfisher*. She was a representative of a class of thirty-four 'streaks' built for the ECML services out of King's Cross with sister *Mallard* achieving fame in 1938 with the never beaten world record for speed with a steam locomotive of 126½mph. I was to catch *Kingfisher* again four months later on her home territory

St Margaret's-allocated ex-LNER A4 No. 60024 *Kingfisher* at Exeter St Davids on 27 March 1966.

A photographic stop at Mortimer on 3 March 1966 with two of the handful of remaining Moguls. Their days were numbered with U No. 31639 being withdrawn that June and N No. 31411 later that month.

A photographic run-past on the Hollywater Loop within the camp at Longmoor with WD196 *Errol Lonsdale* on 16 April 1966.

while working 'The Granite Express' between Aberdeen and Glasgow – she was withdrawn that September.

The Wilts & Hants Rail Tour – Sunday 3 April 1966

Nos 31639 and 31411 – Waterloo (dep 09.15) to Salisbury via Twickenham, Hounslow, Herne Hill, Redhill and Reading; Nos 33006 and 31639 – Salisbury to Waterloo (arr 19.20) via Southampton and Alton = 245¼ miles

Using two of the soon-to-be-withdrawn 'Woolworths', this LCGB tour schedule included a photo stop at Mortimer and sufficient time at Salisbury for a visit to the shed. The Q1 No. 33006 had been officially withdrawn three months earlier but was retained in running order specifically for this tour.

The Longmoor Rail Tour – Sunday 16 April 1966

Nos 31411 and 31639 – Waterloo (dep 10.00) to Woking; WD600 *Gordon* – Woking to Liss; WD600 *Gordon* and WD195 *Sapper* – Liss to Longmoor; WD196 *Errol Lonsdale* – Hollywater Loop; WD600 *Gordon* and WD195 *Sapper* – Longmoor to Bordon; WD600 *Gordon* – Bordon to Staines via Frimley; No. 77014 – Staines to Windsor; Nos 31411 and 31639 – Windsor to Waterloo (arr 19.53) via Hounslow = 139¼ miles

This RCTS tour was so popular a second tour ran two weeks later. The Borden branch had closed to passenger traffic in 1957 and the opportunity to travel within the British Army training camp at Longmoor was rare indeed – *public* passenger services operated by WD (War Department) locomotives being non-existent. WD

WD 195 0–6–0ST *Sapper* and 2–10–0 WD600 *Gordon* at Longmoor on 16 April 1966 preparing to take the tour forward to Bentley. The latter survives today in preservation at the Severn Valley Railway.

600 was a 2–10–0 tender locomotive and WD195/6 were 0–6–0 saddle tanks – usage of the SR's solitary representative of the BR 3MT class, No. 77014, was an additional incentive. The Hollywater loop was a purpose-built circuit within the complex created solely for recruits to gain experience of track laying/lifting procedures – part and parcel of a soldier's requirement when 'invading' the world's trouble spots. The railway closed in 1969 and little trace can be found of it today – an exception being the southern section of Liss which is part of the Royal Woolmer Way footpath.

The A2 Commemorative Tour – Sunday 14 August 1966
No. 60532 *Blue Peter* – Waterloo (dep 09.52) to Westbury via Yeovil & Exeter; No. 70004 *William Shakespeare* –Westbury to Waterloo (arr 21.25) = 358¾ miles

Severe delays (3½ hours) on services into Euston that morning resulting from a landslide in Scotland and a derailment near Watford meant that I arrived with just three minutes to spare at Waterloo. This LCGB tour utilised visiting Dundee-allocated No. 60532 *Blue Peter* – she being one of forty members of ex-LNER A2 Pacifics initially built for the ECML. Not being in the best of condition a very poor run down to Exeter was experienced where, after requiring attention, we left 2½ hours late. The other locomotive used was Stockport-allocated BR 'Britannia' No. 70004 *William Shakespeare*. She was one of fifty-five Pacifics built by BR to replace ageing pre-nationalisation express locomotives and were allocated throughout Britain – No. 70004 herself being exhibited at the Festival of Britain in 1951 and was initially allocated to Stewarts Lane (Battersea) to work the prestige 'Golden Arrow' and 'Night Ferry' services to/from Dover. Like her surviving sisters she had, by 1966, migrated to the north-west of England.

Visiting ex-LNER 4–6–2 A2 No. 60532 *Blue Peter* calls at Axminster for water on 14 August 1966. Note the then-recently closed Lyme Regis branch in the background.

Stockport Edgeley-allocated Brit No. 70004 *William Shakespeare* was deliberately diagrammed to work this 17.23 Southampton Docks departure out of Waterloo on 16 August 1966. This boat train, arranged by enthusiasts in the DMO Wimbledon office to act as a relief to the 17.30 Bournemouth departure conveniently calling at Basingstoke – enabling us cranks to catch her. She had worked into London the previous Sunday (vice the ailing A2) and would return to the LMR via a banana special from Southampton Docks the following day.

The Merchant Navy West Country Tour – Sunday 15 October 1966
No. 35023 *Holland-Afrika Line* – Waterloo to Westbury; No. 35026 *Lamport & Holt Line* – Westbury to Salisbury via Taunton, Exeter & Axminster; No. 35023 *Holland-Afrika Line* – Salisbury to Waterloo (arr 17.20) = 358½ miles

This was an unusual tour in that it was privately sponsored with all profits going to the SR Railwaymen's Home for Children at Woking. A straightforward circular tour, which traversed the WR main line between Westbury and Exeter seven months *after* the WR had rid itself of its own allocation of steam – the eight-coach train being assisted up the 1 in 36 between the Exeter stations by 'Warship' D866 *Zebra*. There was a lot of high-speed running throughout but the highlight of the tour was on the outward leg when Driver Hooker of Nine Elms (having deliberately swapped turns to his financial detriment) attained 101mph down Andover bank. This was my first, out of an eventual four, of speeds in excess of the magic ton behind steam power.

The Shakespearian Rail Tour – Saturday 12 November 1966
No. 34015 *Exmouth* – Waterloo (dep 08.32) to Reading; No. 35023 *Holland-Afrika Line* – Reading to Banbury; No. 7029 *Clun Castle* – Banbury to Stratford; No. 70004 *William Shakespeare* – Stratford to Stourbridge; No. 7029 *Clun Castle* – Stourbridge to Banbury; No. 35023 *Holland-Afrika Line* – Banbury to Victoria (arr 18.57) = 293½ miles

This LCGB tour had Driver Porter driving *Exmouth* on the first leg achieving a seat-grabbing 75mph through Bracknell. No. 7029 *Clun Castle* was a representative of the numerous GWR express 4–6–0s, which powered express services out of

'The Shakespearian Rail Tour' changed locomotives at Banbury on 12 November 1966 from 'Merchant Navy' No. 35023 *Holland-Afrika Line* to the preserved ex-GWR 4–6–0 No. 7029 *Clun Castle*.

There were several 'last' visits by steam to the West Country that year – but this was to be the very last! Standard 5MT 4–6–0 No. 73065 waits for the off at Victoria on 13 November 1966. This ex-ER now Guildford-allocated locomotive was withdrawn from Nine Elms in July 1967.

Paddington. Having worked the final public steam train out of there 1½ years previously, this was her first outing under private ownership.

The West Country Special – Sunday 13 November 1966
No. 73065 – Victoria (dep 09.58) to Westbury via Herne Hill, Redhill and Reading; No. 34019 *Bideford* – Westbury to Yeovil Junction via Taunton and Exeter; No. 35023 *Holland-Afrika Line* – Yeovil Junction to Waterloo (arr 19.42) = 375 miles

This SCTS tour was the *very last* steam to the West Country. The Brunswick green-liveried No. 73029 was booked for the tour but had failed earlier that week with injector problems. Unusually departing out of Victoria the circuitous suburban route included a photograph and water stop at Norwood Junction. After assistance between the two Exeter stations by 'Warship' D818 *Glory Bideford* excelled herself by attaining 86½mph approaching Yeovil on the return leg.

The Bridport Belle Rail Tour – Sunday 22 January 1967
Nos 34102 *Lapford* and 34057 *Biggin Hill* – Waterloo (dep 09.00) to Salisbury via Twickenham and Chertsey; No. 34057 *Biggin Hill* – Salisbury to Westbury; No. 34013 *Okehampton* – Westbury to Maiden Newton; Nos 41295/41320/D6541 – Maiden Newton to Bridport and return; No. 35030 *Elder Dempster Lines* – Maiden Newton to Waterloo (arr 22.25) = 317¾ miles

Many delays befell the participants of this LCGB tour. The first was at North Sheen when the gauge glasses on *Lapford* broke causing the cab to be immediately swamped with steam and boiling water – patched up by the engine crew and Inspector Jupp. The next was an hour's delay at Basingstoke while a 'body' was removed from a toilet – a vagrant having expired overnight after seeking refuge from the cold weather in the stock while berthed at Clapham Yard. On the return journey a mere eight attempts were made at climbing the gradient on the Bridport branch (as described below), the lateness in arrival back into Maiden Newton resulting, after further delay at Sherborne with a block failure, in a direct run from Salisbury to Waterloo instead of the original route via the Pompey direct. Running 214 minutes late at Salisbury an eventual arrival at Waterloo of a 'mere' 149 minutes late was achieved. The following is a summary of the shenanigans on the Bridport branch:

Having arrived at Maiden Newton over an hour late, while the two Ivatt Tanks were being attached at either end of the train 'Merchant Navy' No. 35030, the locomotive that was to take us on our next leg of the tour, arrived from Weymouth – the driver shouting 'come to take you all back to Salisbury.' Upon learning that we hadn't been down the branch yet his response was said to be unprintable before storming off to the signal-box to contact Control as to what do now. It might have occurred to the organisers to cut out the branch visit to regain the schedule but, taking into account the tour was entitled 'The Bridport Belle', it was decided to go ahead. Smart work at Bridport with a reduced turnaround time meant we were only 45 minutes down upon departure back up the 9½-mile branch. The sunny morning had now deteriorated into heavy rain and the combination of greasy rails and nine fully loaded coaches proved too much for the two Class 2MT locomotives and they stalled on the I in 60 gradient between Toller and Powerstock. Several attempts were made with, at one point, the fireman throwing earth onto the running rail

The Unmodified pairing of Nos 34102 *Lapford* and 34057 *Biggin Hill* are seen at the photographic stop on the Salisbury plains at Grateley on 22 January 1967. Can you imagine the health and safety furore if such an event was planned these days?

Ivatt 2–6–2T No. 41320 being coupled to the rear of the tour at Maiden Newton on 22 January 1967 prior to going down the branch to Bridport.

Sister No. 41295 on the stops at Bridport, unaware of the demands about to be placed on her, on 22 January 1967.

and another after setting back to an easier section then taking a run at it – only to stall just short of the summit. Those on board were, initially, loving every minute of it. All windows had heads and tape recorders hanging out of them lapping up the sight and sounds of steam locomotives being worked hard in the many attempts, eventually totalling eight, to breast the summit. Time was moving on and many participants had trains to catch from London up north and enjoyment gradually turned to concern.

At 15.55, the drivers finally admitted defeat. They were mentally exhausted, their engines – especially No. 41320 in the lead – were well and truly winded, and the carriages and couplings had taken a terrible hammering with the constant violent jolting. With No. 41295 running dangerously short of water the decision was made, between the train crews and the organisers, to turn off the steam heating to the train enabling boiler pressure on No. 41295 to be reduced to an absolute minimum and send the other loco (itself pretty low on water) and three coaches off to Maiden Newton to summon help. This plan had to be abandoned when it proved impossible to uncouple the coaches safely on the gradient and so the front loco was sent off on its own at 16.20 – weight restrictions on the branch line meaning that the 'Merchant Navy', which hopefully was still waiting at Maiden Newton, could not be used for the rescue. We were effectively left stranded seemingly in the middle of nowhere. No lights from nearby farms were visible and, with no heat, it was gradually getting colder until – much to the chagrin of all the steam buffs on board, our rescuer, in the form of Type 3 Crompton D6541 arrived on the scene. She soon coupled up but was unable, on her own, to get a grip on the wet rails – the smell of wheel spin and overheating electrical wiring filling the air. Ivatt No. 41295, at the rear with her precious little reserve of water, was requisitioned back into action and, with all ears covered in case her boiler exploded, together with the diesel finally pushed us over the top – with ALL wheels spinning on both traction units! We arrived back into Maiden Newton, where thankfully the 'Merchant Navy' was still waiting, 3 hours and 10 minutes late.

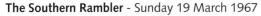

The Southern Rambler - Sunday 19 March 1967
No. 34108 *Wincanton* – Victoria (dep 11.02) to Victoria (arr 17.26) via Lewisham, Selsdon, East Croydon, Brighton and Eastbourne = 144¾ miles

On the preceding Friday I had attended a meeting at Birmingham in the course of duty (pigeon traffic arrangements) then headed straight into an overnight bash on the Bournemouth line, briefly visiting home for a wash and brush up on the Saturday evening before then catching the 03.30 Waterloo to Portsmouth Harbour Papers on the Sunday morning of the tour. Being unusually diverted via Epsom and Dorking resulting from engineering works, the train locomotive No. 34052 *Lord Dowding,* having been delayed en route, then ran out of water at Fratton – was replaced, departed 84 minutes late and diverted into the Southsea terminus, with Standard Tank No. 80152. The journey itself was most agreeable. As dawn was breaking, the beautiful Sussex countryside was seen in all its glory. It was made even more pleasurable courtesy of the wide-windowed Bulleid compartment – myself the only passenger. Returning to London via the Pompey Direct on a rail replacement bus service en route, to say I was knackered upon boarding the tour would have been an understatement! This SCTS tour, which was the very last steam train to the Sussex coast, covered the Elmers End to Selsdon line, which closed in

A pairing of ex-SR USA 0–6–0Ts, Nos 30064 and 30069 at Southampton Central on 9 April 1967.

1983, part of which is used by the Croydon Tramlink system. At Selsdon Class 73 Electro-diesel E6016 hauled the train back to East Croydon and at Brighton Class 08 diesel shunter D3219 worked the train from Signal CB71 (outside the station) into the platform – thus avoiding *Wincanton* becoming trapped.

The Hampshire Branch Lines Rail Tour – Sunday 9 April 1967
No. 35023 *Holland-Afrika Line* – Waterloo (dep 09.21) to Salisbury; No. 34057 *Biggin Hill* – Salisbury to Southampton Central via Chandler's Ford; Nos 30064 and 30069 – Southampton Central to Totton via Fawley; No. 80151 – Totton to Brockenhurst; Nos 80151 and 41320 – Brockenhurst to Lymington and return; No. 34025 *Whimple* – Brockenhurst to Ascot via Reading; No. 76031 – Ascot to Aldershot via Frimley; No. 77014 – Aldershot to Guildford; No. 73093 – Guildford to Waterloo (arr 21.05) = 293¾ miles.

This LCGB tour used ten different locomotives – a fantastic organisational achievement. The main attraction was the usage of the USA engines normally confined to Southampton Docks along the now freight-only Fawley branch. An attempt was made to reduce the late running by eliminating a photographic stop at Mortimer, but a 55-minute late arrival still was collected.

The Dorset Coast Express Rail Tour – Sunday 7 May 1967
No. 34021 *Dartmoor* – Waterloo (dep 09.13) to Wareham via Havant; No. 34023 *Blackmore Vale* and No. 76026 – Wareham to Swanage and return; No. 34023 *Blackmore Vale* and No. 80011 – Wareham to Swanage and return; No. 34023 *Blackmore Vale* – Wareham to Weymouth; Nos 76026 and 73029 – Weymouth to Bournemouth Central; No. 35003 *Royal Mail* – Bournemouth Central to Waterloo (arr 20.09) = 341¾ miles

Water stop at Fareham on 7 May 1967 with 'West Country' No. 34021 *Dartmoor*. Two further 108-mile runs with her within a week just pushed my mileage with her over the magic 1,000.

One of only two Unmodified 'Spam Cans' which lasted until July 1967 was No. 34023 *Blackmore Vale* – seen here on a photographic run past at Corfe Castle on 7 May 1967.

Withdrawn from Aberdeen in March 1966 the now-preserved No. 4498 (60007) *Sir Nigel Gresley* visits Bournemouth on 3 June 1967.

This LCGB tour went without a hitch. A unique, at the time, double run on the Swanage branch was operated for photographic purposes with Corfe Castle as the backdrop. All those who wanted a photograph alighted from the train and stood alongside the track while the train reversed to some distance away. Then, with whistle blowing and a deliberately black-smoked scenario created, the train stormed by, stopping some distance further up the line before once again reversing to allow us to reboard the train. Today's health and safety officers would have had heart attacks! A very lively run from Weymouth to Bournemouth with the two Standards peaked at 78mph at the approach to the junction for the Swanage branch at Worgret.

Farewell to Southern Steam Tour – Sunday 18 June 1967
Nos 73029 and 34023 *Blackmore Vale* – Waterloo (dep 10.57) to Fareham via East Putney, Guildford New Line and Havant; No. 34089 *602 Squadron* – Fareham to Southampton Central; No. 34108 *Wincanton* and No. 34089 *602 Squadron* – Southampton Central to Wareham; No. 34089 *602 Squadron* and No. 80146 – Wareham to Swanage and return; No. 34089 *602 Squadron* – Wareham to Weymouth; No. 34089 *602 Squadron* and No. 34023 *Blackmore Vale* – Weymouth to Salisbury via Chandler's Ford; No. 35013 *Blue Funnel* – Salisbury to Waterloo = 350½ miles

Having spent two overnights in the north-west, an arrival time into Euston of 06.25 gave me ample time to catch this RCTS Tour. This was the second (of three) dates for the cessation of steam on the SR – the original being the previous April. Further delay in the provision of new stock put the date back another four weeks but this tour still went ahead as planned. General late running caused a 55-minute late arrival back into London.

15

WESSEX WANDERINGS

A steam train made the national news on Saturday 18 June 2005 when, for the first time in thirty-eight years, preserved 'Battle of Britain' No. 34067 *Tangmere*, worked a titled train under the banner of 'The Royal Wessex' from Weymouth to London. The original Southern Region 'Royal Wessex' first ran in 1951 as part of the Festival of Britain celebrations – the ancient kingdom of Wessex having been brought to prominence a century earlier by the novels of 'local' Thomas Hardy. The kingdom was devoid of any fixed borders, its boundaries being dictated by those loyal to the king. As such it is hard to define the exact geographical location but the *Encyclopaedia Britannica* lists the counties of Hampshire, Somerset, Dorset and Wiltshire as the 'permanent' nucleus of the Kingdom of Wessex upon which this chapter is centred. As a fair percentage of my steam chasing occurred within this area I would now like to take the reader with me on a sweep of the Wessex area from the south-east at Portsmouth then through Hampshire to Dorset.

Pompey-bound

Portsmouth had been well-served from the 1930s by the Southern's 'Electric Coast' – a wonderfully descriptive advertising slogan highlighting the 261 route miles of electric train services radiating from London to Hastings, Brighton and Portsmouth. Visits to Portsmouth by steam were, for me, rare and it wasn't until May 1965, with the imminent dieselisation of the cross-country Cardiff trains the following month, that I travelled on several services behind Salisbury-allocated BR Standard 4MTs into and out of the naval city. Initially travelling from Victoria to Barnham via the Mid-Sussex route (via Horsham) connected into the 10.25 Brighton to Plymouth service which, as far as Chichester, was worked by electric locomotive E5013. Twenty-four examples of these 25,552hp locomotives, primarily constructed for post-steam Kent freight services in addition to replacing steam on the prestige 'Night Ferry' and 'Golden Arrow' services, were built during 1958. At Chichester, Unmodified Pacific No. 34066 *Spitfire* took over for the 58½-mile run to Salisbury calling at Fareham where a 76xxx was waiting on the truncated Gosport branch stub, with the Portsmouth portion, which she attached at the rear. At Salisbury I didn't have to wait long before the 10.35 Cardiff to Portsmouth service arrived – the WR Hymek diesel giving way to Standard Mogul 76018 with which I retraced my steps back to Romsey. Travelling over to Eastleigh via Chandler's Ford, a route closed to passengers four years later but subsequently reopened in 2003, I then briefly visited Winchester before catching the opposite way working of the daily Plymouth to Brighton train travelled upon earlier that day. Now, however, to travel into Portsmouth by steam I deliberately positioned myself in the rear portion, which upon detachment at Fareham was worked forward by tender-first Nine Elms Standard No. 73086 *The Green Knight*. She was in what can only be described as a deplorable condition with name and numberplates missing and rust in profusion. She must have, however, been mechanically sound because she lasted a further fourteen months! A cup of tea and another run with a 76xxx on a Cardiff service as far as Fratton before travelling home up the Pompey Direct, naturally changing at Woking onto a steam service, completed a very satisfactory day with runs behind nine different steam locomotives. It was a further eighteen months before a steam arrival, on the 02.30 Papers from Waterloo, into the harbour station while en route to the Isle of Wight was achieved.

As covered in chapter eleven, chasing particular engines for mileage accumulation became a way of life for similarly minded enthusiasts and to this end on two further occasions, solely for that purpose, I was aboard the same service. Soon after the

Two weeks before the dieselisation of the services, Eastleigh's Standard Mogul No. 76016 waits at Portsmouth & Southsea on 22 May 1965 with the 17.45 departure for Cardiff Central. She was to be transferred to Guildford, and was withdrawn from there in October 1966.

The diversity of steam classes witnessed at Basingstoke can be seen over the next few photographs. Oxford's Modified Hall No. 6991 *Acton Burnell Hall* runs light engine past the old ex-GWR platforms at Basingstoke on 11 September 1965 – her days finishing with the WR cull of steam three months later.

05.39 arrival at Portsmouth Harbour the locomotive propelled the stock back to the carriage sidings at Fratton where, having been serviced and turned, once again propelled the same stock back into Portsmouth to form the 07.30 to Eastleigh – a service predominantly run for workers at the vast locomotive works there. It was on this train that I obtained the 'magic' 1,000 miles behind both en route – they being 'West Country' No. 34108 *Wincanton* and, in the final week of steam, sister No. 34036 *Westward Ho!*

Basingstoke to the Dorset coast

The 143-mile line from Waterloo to Weymouth played a major part in my steam travels, without which I would never have accumulated such fantastically high steam mileages. Perhaps the most visited station was Basingstoke at 47¾ miles from Waterloo. Back then it was a town of just 30,000 inhabitants but together with a new futuristic shopping centre opened in 1969 and the area being designated as a London overspill town, the resultant massive increase in commuting to the capital is enjoyed by its now *c.* 80,000 inhabitants. Railway-wise it was an important junction between the LSWR main lines to the west of England and Bournemouth routes and the Reading line – the latter enabling Inter-Regional services, both passenger and freight, access from throughout Britain to southern destinations. Although by 1966 no passenger services were booked to change traction there, having its own motive power depot with its attendant availability of locomotives and crews made it a natural engine-changing point for trains in trouble – the four running lines being a significant operational advantage with the ability for following services to pass by. Perhaps here I can relate some travelling 'delays' at this location as examples of such occasions. On one afternoon in March 1966 I had travelled down to Dorchester on 'The Royal Wessex' (16.35 ex-Waterloo), having negotiated an early departure from work because I was chasing 'Merchant Navy' No. 35012 at the time, and after completing a local bash in the Poole area was returning on the overnight Up Mails – falling asleep en route. A slammed door must have awoken me and upon suddenly realising I was at Woking and not wanting to become stranded in London at such an ungodly hour, I leapt off and dashed over the footbridge, being challenged in my semi-comatose state by a BT policeman as to where I was going in such a hurry at that time of the morning (it was 3.00 a.m.) and jumped aboard the 02.45 Papers ex-Waterloo – which had just received the 'right away' signal – not knowing what was at the front. At Basingstoke I found out when 'West Country' No. 34025 *Whimple* was detached, her driver having declared her a failure, and taken on to the shed. Without any heat on that cold March morning we sat in the platform awaiting our rescuer, gradually getting colder and colder before 'Battle of Britain' No. 34052 *Lord Dowding* eventually took us forward an hour later – no doubt all the newsagents waiting at the stations throughout Hampshire suffering similarly! Four days later and the fireman on No. 34040, which was working the 10.30 Waterloo to Weymouth, somehow broke or lost his shovel and so an additional stop at Basingstoke was made. Returning to the train, having successfully obtained a replacement, he noticed a hot box on *Crewkerne's* tender – twenty-five minutes later the Class 1 service being taken forward by the hastily prepared Standard No. 75077.

On another occasion a somewhat unusual sight greeted me when, upon arrival into Basingstoke just days before Christmas that year on a Down commuter train,

A frosty
28 December 1965
at Basingstoke sees
Stoke's ex-LMS 8F
2–8–0 No. 48453
running light engine
towards Reading.
Her days ended at
Patricroft in April
1968.

Austerity 8F 2–8–0
No. 90295 of
Stavely Barrow
Hill at Basingstoke
making a surprise
visit to the SR on
11 September
1965 with an
Eastleigh-bound
freight of bogie
bolsters.

Banbury's BR 9F
2–10–0 No. 92132
crawls through
Basingstoke on
2 July 1965, having
been checked by
signals. She was to
be transferred to
Carlisle Kingmoor
being withdrawn
upon that shed's
closure to steam in
December 1967.

It wasn't unusual for foremen to utilise visiting locomotives from other depots when the booked locomotive was failed – Salisbury's Light Pacific No. 34100 *Appledore* found herself working the 12.57 Bournemouth Central to Waterloo on 11 December 1965, seen here calling at Basingstoke.

'The Bournemouth Belle' was noted in the Up platform full of passengers tucking into their high tea – without an engine! Eventually Standard No. 73018 took the train forward an hour late.

Finally still at Basingstoke, but not an engine change, a lifetime ambition was achieved when I (together with several other colleagues) genuinely pulled the communication cord because the driver on No. 34018 *Axminster* working the 17.23 Waterloo to Southampton Docks failed to remember that on this night (14 June 1967) the service was advertised as a relief to the 17.30 Bournemouth. He was accelerating through the station, having been checked by signals outside, but managed to stop with the rear two vehicles still on the platform – continuing after a slight delay with all the butterflies (external indicators of vacuum brake loss on the coach side) having been reset.

So now we begin a trip down the main Bournemouth route. At 58 miles from Waterloo the first station we come across is Micheldever, originally named Andover Road, and situated 2 miles north of the village high up on the Hampshire grass downland. It was from here, in 1895, that the first recorded journey by car (to Datchet) in the UK took place – it having been imported from France and delivered by rail via Southampton docks. Surrounded by a wall of chalk in a cutting, it was the location of both an oil terminal and a number of sidings at which condemned rolling stock was stored, presumably awaiting destruction at Eastleigh. Micheldever was often passed at speed and I was to set foot on the island platform just once; the purpose of which was to obtain a run behind my last-required SR allocated locomotive – No. 76007. They say that during your career you often only remember the mistakes made rather than the successes. When I was working in the Special Traffic Section at DMO Wimbledon as a lowly graded clerk, one of my duties was to time the light engine requirements for the Engine Diagrams section. On one occasion they wanted a pathway from Basingstoke to Eastleigh which, using the relevant graphs, I supplied them with. What I had failed to take into consideration was that there was an engineering possession in the area and the light steam locomotive could get no further than the nearby (to Micheldever) loop at Wallers Ash. The train crew had to drop the fire and get a taxi home with a fresh crew the following day retrieving the abandoned locomotive – the water being supplied from the signal-box. On the Monday morning I was hauled before my boss and admonished appropriately!

We now move on 4¼ miles to Winchester Junction. Perhaps these days passengers passing the site of the junction encapsulated within their air-conditioned sleek EMUs can, if they are quick enough, just glimpse the gap in the foliage where the former route to Alton, closed in 1973, can be seen. Back in the 1960s the regulation of the hourly service off of the Alton line was vital in respect of a clear road for the southbound expresses on the main line to obtain the fast speeds down the bank often achieved in the final months. Other than rail tours I was to travel 'over the Alps' (an appropriate description of the route between Alton and Winchester as it had to negotiate the North Downs) only twice with steam and unfortunately on both occasions 'suffering' diesel pilot assistance either from Woking or Alton – it being a vital diversionary route during the electrification work. Some of my colleagues were more fortunate, because on some of their trips the often diverted steam services obtained assistance with the Guildford-allocated sole BR 2–6–0 3MT – No. 77014. The original intention of transferring the remaining numbers of that class, they were a mere twelve years old and therefore in reasonable condition, from throughout Britain never materialised – presumably because the need for steam power was ever decreasing as more modern forms of motive power were drafted in. I sometimes return to the now-preserved section so excellently run by the Mid Hants Railway Preservation Society (Watercress Line) between Alton and Alresford. With its steep gradients and the society's penchant for often using Pacific locomotives, an accurate portrayal of the power the steam locomotive can muster is recreated. I am surprisingly STILL catching trains with new (to me) locomotives on them courtesy of the organisation's policy of hiring them from other railways elsewhere throughout Britain.

Returning to the main line I recorded many high-speed descents down the bank into Winchester – where most expresses called. I would have thought that the signal-box at the junction was caked in brake dust as it was at that point where the anchors were slammed on – Winchester station being a very short distance away. I was aboard the 08.35 Waterloo to Weymouth train when Driver Parsons (Nine Elms) with 'Merchant Navy' No. 35012 and a load of ten coaches achieved 94mph at the junction during the April of 1967. For sheer consistency, however, Driver Porter of 70A was renowned for 'coaxing' the best out of the locomotives in his charge. 'The Bournemouth Belle', an all-Pullman car train introduced by the LSWR in 1890 and suspended during the two world wars, was caught on New Year's Eve 1966 and Porter pushed Light Pacific No. 34093 *Saunton* up to 86mph through Shawford – one of the few services deigning not to call at Winchester. Everything in the elderly Pullmans rattled, with cutlery and china becoming 'somewhat mobile'. Porter's comment at Southampton was merely 'the b*****d just doesn't go!' – still well worth the supplement.

Heading up the bank just three weeks later on the 17.30 ex-Weymouth with sister engine No. 34036 *Westward Ho!* I have never witnessed a fireworks display

On 21 March 1967 Salisbury's No. 76008 storms away from Eastleigh with the 08.29 stopper for Bournemouth Central. Note the conductor rails in situ in readiness for electric services to commence that July.

from a Bulleid like it – due apparently to a faulty spark arrester. Shooting stars descended all over the place with (I read in the control log later) numerous lineside fires being started.

The Hampshire town of Eastleigh, 73½ miles from Waterloo, was, together with the likes of Ashford, Swindon, and Crewe, etc., a railway town. The largest employer in the area was Eastleigh Works, which, resulting from the transfer of locomotive construction from Nine Elms in 1910, became the axis of the motive power fleet for the L&SWR/Southern Railway/latter day South-Western Division of the Southern Region. Eastleigh shed, although the largest on the SR, still never surpassed the sheer size and smokescreen of Crewe South. Observed at night from a carriage window of a Euston train I had never seen such a scene of tower lights, steam, and smoke drifting over what seemed like the entire landscape. Eastleigh station, initially Bishopstoke when opened in 1839, was only served by a handful of expresses from London but was compensated with a great many local stopping services – only some of which were steam-operated. Rarely visited by myself I sometimes, with time to kill while awaiting express services at Southampton, made a fill-in trip on local services if a required engine was circulating. Other than that on a couple of occasions I arrived at the unearthly hour of 00.45 off of the Down Mails and was eyed with suspicion while I 'hung around' for the 02.02 WR Hymek departure for Salisbury and the west.

Heading further south the then recently opened Southampton Airport, in those days just a pair of concrete alighting points, is passed before reaching the city of Southampton itself which once upon a time was served by two stations – the first opened being Southampton Terminus, 79 miles from Waterloo, in 1839. As befitting its importance as the main and terminal station for the growing city it was built in the Italianate style and subsequently (in 1891) provided with six platforms. It, however, lost its importance with the greater travelling opportunities being available at the 'new' Southampton West and, although more centrally located by the time I visited it, the only trains serving it were the hourly local services from Alton and irregular Bournemouth stopping services. Not being included within the electrification programme it was closed in September 1966 but still survives today because of its listed status – albeit as a casino. I only visited there on two occasions. The first, in September 1965, was essentially a track bash when, having arrived on a DEMU service originating from Alton, I then caught Mogul No. 76014 working the 16.12 stopper to Bournemouth. The other was just weeks away from its closure when the Up Mails was booked to call (reverse) there – a somewhat curious engine working being uncovered on that occasion. The train engine No. 34040 *Crewkerne*, which had worked in to Southampton Central from Weymouth, was detached and disappeared into the tunnel east of the station to Northam. A tender first Light Pacific No. 34012 *Launceston* then suddenly appeared, coupled up and drew the train the short distance to the terminus station where, lo and behold, the original *Crewkerne* reappeared and proceeded to work forward to Waterloo. Years later, while reading an article on the Mail train locomotive diagrams, I learned that *Crewkerne*'s next duty was to take the Down Mails forward to Weymouth upon reversal of that train at Southampton Terminus – a changeover location for the travelling GPO staff between Up/Down Mail services. Southampton Central (née West) when opened in 1895 was built on the seafront and as such, until the land reclamation scheme of 1927 during which the nearby docks complex was constructed, was subject to frequent flooding. Redeveloped and expanded during the 1930s, when the end of steam came further building alterations took place resulting in the notable 100ft high clock tower, which nowadays would have qualified for a conservation order, being demolished in favour of the inevitable office block.

Many non-stop trains to London were boarded here with not-always-realised expectations of high-speed running en route. In the opposite direction the local stopping services to the New Forest and Bournemouth were often jumped upon if 'required' locomotives were at the helm – healthily contributing to my catches.

Onwards we go – just a short distance to the junction station of Totton from which the 9¾-mile Fawley line branched off. Opened as late as 1925 specifically to serve the recently built oil refinery, at the branch's terminus the passenger service provided was always only for those workers. Friday 11 February 1966 was the last day of the twice daily (SX) passenger service – this was to be my first 'last' train. Formed of 3H DEMU 1128 the 16.01 departure from Southampton Central was crowded but the return 16.48 was full and standing even in the first class section where I was privileged to be! Several signalmen at boxes en route had placed detonators on the line, which added to the sense of occasion. Alighting

Eastleigh-allocated Modified Pacific No. 34095 *Brentnor* rests at Southampton Central on 11 February 1965 while working the 11.30 Waterloo to Bournemouth Central. She was to work the final 02.45 departure out of Waterloo but even driver Porter couldn't get a ton out of her!

Fawley, after the arrival of the final passenger train on 11 February 1966 – the 15.46 from Eastleigh. The return train (there were only two per day) was accompanied by detonators placed at various places along the route.

at the junction station of Totton I was among numerous enthusiasts who went to the ticket office to ascertain if old Southern Railway tickets were still available in his stock. There were, and we were sold tickets for Hythe and Fawley AFTER the last train had gone! The souvenir aspect was catered for, however, because it had the last day's date on it. The only other occasion I visited the line was on 'The Hampshire Lines' rail tour on Sunday 9 April 1967 when two 'USA' 0–6–0Ts, Nos 30064 and 30069, worked probably the longest (ten vehicles) passenger train that

BR Standard 5MT No. 73170 departing Lyndhurst Road on 11 February 1965 with the 14.02 Eastleigh to Bournemouth Central.

The 13.57 Bournemouth Central to Southampton Terminus arrives into Lyndhurst Road on 11 February 1965 with Bournemouth's Standard Mogul No. 76026 in charge. I sometimes, while awaiting main line services at Southampton, popped along to these New Forest stations in a bid to catch runs with locomotives not usually found on Waterloo trains.

ever visited the branch. These locos were part of a batch of fourteen bought by the Southern Railway from an American WD dump at Newbury racecourse sidings in 1946. Having travelled by car in the area over recent years I am astonished that a passenger service has not been reinstated – the line still in use because of continued use by freight traffic. The subsequently expanded mini-towns of Dibden Purlieu and Marchwood I would have thought could create sufficient passenger demand – indeed it is one of the proposed twenty town/line reinstatements proposed by ATOC. The New Forest intermediate stations such as Lyndhurst Road, Hinton Admiral and Sway, while much appreciated and used by numerous holidaymakers and tourists visiting what has become Britain's newest National Park, were only utilised by myself to achieve the aforementioned catches. Unlike today where a regular interval stopping service calls at them, back then there very long gaps and care had to be taken not to get stranded for an hour or two – while witnessing the fast trains, perhaps even the ones I originally had planned to travel on, speed through. Just because I wanted Mogul No. 76006 I even suffered noisy and unruly schoolchildren on the 16.03 (Unadvertised – Schooldays Only) Brockenhurst to Christchurch service one day in January 1967.

Having just enjoyed a run with Guildford's BR 5MT No. 73117 *Vivien* I alighted at Brockenhurst in order to catch a 'required' tank on the Lymington branch allowing her to continue to Bournemouth Central with the 11.30 ex-Waterloo. Note the 'Ron Cover' makeshift wooden smokebox numberplate.

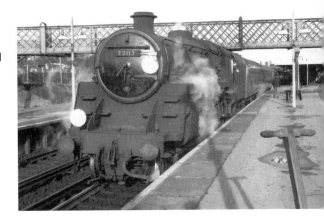

A cold, miserable winter morning (18 January 1967) at Sway sees Light Pacific No. 34108 *Wincanton* departing with the 08.46 semi-fast Bournemouth Central to Waterloo. I had caught this service the 12½ miles from Bournemouth to here to tip my mileage with *Wincanton* over the magic 1,000.

Having heard through the grapevine that a Blackie had headed westward with a special from Loughborough earlier that day, I wasn't at all surprised to see this interloper at Christchurch on 3 July 1965. Ex-LMS Stanier 4–6–0 5MT No. 45349 of Northampton, was returning light engine to the LMR that afternoon – I was to catch her on the ex-GC Marylebone services that December.

Moving southwards along the main line through the New Forest we now arrive at Bournemouth. The Central station, 108 miles from Waterloo, originally opened as the East in 1885. It changed its name when it became a through-station three years later, and was designed with wonderful ornate metalwork and a glazed panelled windscreen at each end which regrettably fell into disrepair as a result of damage incurred during the 1987 hurricane. Full restoration was eventually achieved following monies gained from conservation and heritage means. Bournemouth (as it is NOW known) has one of the longest station platforms in Britain – the country (Poole) end of which enabled the visitor to view most of the locomotives on the shed and, to which I made two visits (Appendix IV) without the necessary permit, managing to avoid the usual 'clear off' (or worse) vitriol from the foreman. The site, as with so much steam age infrastructure, has become the inevitable car park. In steam days the station was always a hive of activity with restaurant car portions being attached or detached going onto or from the West station, a station pilot (initially M7s – latterly Ivatts) always simmering in the centre road and of course the inevitable excitement generated when either a diesel failed or an Inter-Regional service turned up with unusual motive power.

Bournemouth seafront or cliff top playing fields were frequented on Sundays having arrived on the 09.33 excursion or 11.30 departures from Waterloo by an ever-expanding group of enthusiasts while waiting for whatever returning steam services to the capital. Games of footy on a green at the top of Bournemouth cliffs were often enjoyed and on one occasion the distant chimes of a visiting LNER A4

On 4 February 1967 BR Standard 4MT No. 80019 sits in the middle road at Bournemouth Central with the stock to form the 17.02(SX) for Wareham. This service originally used to go through to Swanage but DEMUs had taken over branch services in September 1966, thus truncating this train. Note the lengthy platform there – ideal for observing action at the motive power depot opposite.

We came from all walks of life. Some railway men, some not. The common denominator was haulage by steam. Season ticket holders and overnight bashers – we were there for the mileages. Great companionship – some lasting until the present day. Bournemouth cliffs (just west of the pier) was a place for a game of footy while waiting for the returning steam services to Waterloo on a Sunday. From left to right: Roger Blundell, -?-, Paul (Plittle) Little, Bob (Doze) Thompson, Paul Howard, Andrew (Clackers) Clarke, John (Shunter) Braybrooke, Les (Lurch) Kent, Keith (Wild Bill) Widdowson, Alan (Nobby) Hayes, -?-,Tony (Banks) Lever, Richard (Joe) Jolliffee, Andrew Malphus and Adrian Berridge. There were a great many more but alas I have no photographic record of you – apologies. (Photographer unknown)

Closure of Bournemouth West Station

Bus service between Bournemouth Central and Bournemouth West

6 September to 3 October 1965

MONDAYS TO SATURDAYS

DOWN			UP		
Train due	Connecting bus departs Bournemouth Central	Connecting bus arrives Bournemouth West	Connecting bus departs Bournemouth West	Connecting bus arrives Bournemouth Central	Train departs
08 32	08 37	08 52	06 37 SX	06 52 SX	07 02 SX
10 45 SX	10 50 SX	11 05 SX	06 59	07 14	07 24
11 29	11 34	11 49	07 12	07 27	07 37
12 36	12 41	12 56	08 10	08 25	08 35
12 45	12 50	13 05	08 21	08 36	08 46
14 30	14 35	14 50	08 59	09 14	09 24
14 45	14 50	15 05	09 41	09 56	10 06
15 02 SO	15 07 SO	15 22 SO	10 03	10 18	10 28
15 27 SX	15 32 SX	15 47 SX	10 31	10 46	10 56
15 37 SO	15 42 SO	15 57 SO	10 42	10 57	11 07
16 28	16 33	16 48	12 09	12 24	12 34
16 43	16 48	17 03	12 34	12 49	12 59
17 59 SX	18 04 SX	18 19 SX	14 10	14 25	14 35
18 31 SX	18 37	18 52	14 44	14 59	15 09
18 32 SO			16 12	16 27	16 37
18 52	18 57	19 12	16 46	17 03	17 13
19 02 FO	19 14	19 29	18 10	18 25	18 35
19 09			18 26	18 41	18 51
20 07 FO	20 12 FO	20 27 FO			
20 28	20 33	20 48	FO—Fridays only.		
20 44 FO	20 49 FO	21 04 FO	SO—Saturdays only.		
20 52	20 57	21 12			
22 25			SX—Saturdays excepted.		
22 41	22 46	23 01			

SUNDAYS

DOWN			UP		
11 47	11 52	12 07	09 09	09 24	09 34
12 38	12 43	12 58	10 09	10 24	10 34
12 57	13 02	13 17	10 46	11 01	11 11
14 23	14 28	14 43	13 04	13 19	13 29
14 45	14 50	15 05	14 00	14 15	14 25
15 11	15 16	15 31	15 08	15 23	15 33
16 22	16 27	16 42	15 46	16 01	16 11
18 16	18 21	18 36	16 12	16 27	16 37
19 19	19 28	19 43	17 47	18 02	18 12
21 39	21 44	21 59	18 29	18 44	18 54
22 03	22 08	22 23	19 11	19 26	19 36
23 34	23 39	23 54	20 03	20 18	20 28
			21 14	21 29	21 39

See overleaf for bus services between Branksome and Bournemouth West

A closure pamphlet signifying the demise of Bournemouth West.

Storming away from Bournemouth West on the evening of 3 July 1965 is Bournemouth's No. 76057 on the 18.48 for Templecombe.

Unbelievably my only (steam) shot at Weymouth. On 3 June 1967 nameless 'West Country' No. 34034 formerly *Honiton* awaits departure with the 17.00 vans for Waterloo.

Pacific could be heard! As a variation we sometimes all took boats out on Poole boating lake – never to be forgotten occasions and certainly never able to be repeated. With steam finished we all disappeared to our respective parts of the country and, had Facebook been around in those days, perhaps more contact could have been maintained. Since retiring, with work commitments being dispensed with, I occasionally meet up with some of those friends, always involving regular conversational opening lines of 'do you remember so and so?' or, 'what about the time we . . . ?' – as no doubt most reunions of groups from all walks of life discuss.

At 111½ miles from Waterloo, Bournemouth West station, opened in 1874 (from the Poole direction), was an effective alternative to the congested Central – with services to Bath, Bristol and a myriad of local destinations. The station lay at the foot of an incline from the main line junction station of Branksome and trains heading out of the station not only had to contend with a 1 in 90 gradient but also a curvature of 300 degrees. The distance by rail between West and Central stations was 3½ miles but as the crow flies it was less than half that. Interestingly this was only one of two (the other being Weymouth) coastal terminus built to main line standards thus allowing Bulleid's magnificent, but heavy, 'Merchant Navy' class to work from them. Some semi-fast services to Waterloo started from here but, although better positioned within the town, and a mere five-minute walk away from the seafront, the terminus was closed by the usual method of stealth in the autumn of 1965. Initially services to the west were diverted to the Central in August 'due to engineering work in connection with the electrification'. Then the services to the east were replaced by a bus service in the September and BR, realising it could cater for ALL train services without the need for the West station, decided to close the station forever!

Moving ever further west we come to the tightly curved Poole station, at 113¾ miles from Waterloo, which has undergone many rebuilding alterations since steam days and can now take twelve-car services – with further plans to move it westwards and to incorporate it within a transport interchange hub. Again only occasionally using it, I do remember a cacophony of bells and semaphore signal movements always taking place to herald the arrival of a train from the Bournemouth direction. The reason being the need to close two sets of level crossing gates and the resultant chaos to both foot and vehicular traffic immediately to the east of the station – the road traffic nowadays using a new over bridge.

West of Poole the isolated Holton Heath Halt was only stood upon for a mere 14 minutes – just three weeks before the cessation of steam. Opened during the First World War to enable workers at the adjacent Royal Naval Cordite factory to commute there, it was not shown in a public timetable until 1924 – perhaps for security purposes. When the factory closed in 1959 an industrial estate was built and an astonishing 30,000 (ORR figures) passengers per year now use the 'platform'. The objective for my visit back then, precisely as with my only visit to Micheldever, was for exactly the same reason and the same train. One of my last required Standard Moguls, this time No. 76067, was working the 16.46 Weymouth to Woking all stations train – and having ascertained the fact she was working the service I travelled down on the 17.02 from Bournemouth to catch her. This was originally a Swanage service but with the dieselisation of branch services by DEMUs this train, now terminating at Wareham, was powered by one of the then new EDLs. The nearby Hamworthy goods branch, although sometimes the destination of railtours was, alas, only visited by myself using road transport as part of my wagon auditing duties – a wonderful three-month long 'away from the desk' position held at DMO Wimbledon as a result of one of the many reorganisational changes endured throughout my career. What did it involve – merely visiting often-remote locations to ensure the details submitted by the responsible railwaymen was a true reflection of what was on site.

Anyway, back to the route and now we come to the end of the line at Weymouth – 143 miles from Waterloo. Having briefly visited in April 1964 it wasn't until July 1965 that I returned. A very pleasant town, often subsequently visited when staying in the area, the approach by rail was down an escarpment offering panoramic views of Weymouth Bay, the summit of which was at Bincombe, before descending to sea level in a mere 4 miles. On the July visit I was to stay a mere thirty-five minutes – the objective of travelling on the 11.05 cross-country departure for Wolverhampton. This service was one of the few remaining steam passenger services via Yeovil and Swindon to Oxford where the SR-based locomotive (No. 73020) came off. A wonderful cross-country journey through by then diesel-infested Wiltshire passing through Swindon – the one-time pivotal HQ of Brunel's Great Western Railway empire.

Passing through Wareham we come to the curiously laid-out Dorchester South station (at which London-bound services had to reverse into until rebuilding in 1989, a legacy of the original ownership which had aspirations of continuing westwards on a coastal route to Exeter) was reached on three occasions in January and February on the 13.30 ex-Waterloo (due 17.26) and returning on the 17.30 Weymouth departing 17.46 – 7½ hours of travelling for 271½ miles of steam and just a 20-minute break – mad or what? What did I do to pass the time you may wonder? With the express services always having a buffet, food and drink was always readily available and sleeping, reading and recording the passing times and speeds was balanced with looking out of the window for passing steam at depots or on other trains. By always travelling in the coach closest to the locomotive, I could occasionally lean out of the window (in those days not being entombed within a plastic pipe) and listen to it working hard. As there were seemingly always like-minded colleagues travelling on these services, exchanging information also filled the time.

After only visiting Weymouth on one occasion during 1966 while chasing 'Merchant Navy' No. 35008 *Orient Line* when she worked the 22.13 Up Mails to Waterloo, we move on to 1967 when some serious mileage accumulation trips were made. To this end, with an ever-reducing amount of locomotives in circulation, and, with the arrival of the six Brush Type 4 diesels specifically allocated to the SR thus reducing the booked trains on which steam was scheduled, it became easier by having selected the required locomotive just to follow her on her diagram on whatever services she worked.

Time was running out and on the first Saturday of that June, having completed two nights out on trains 'oop north' I spent the day on SR services ending up on the 17.30 Weymouth to Waterloo. Catching it out of Weymouth, being a lengthy train (those exceeding five vehicles necessitated assistance) the train engine, No. 34001 *Exeter*, was noisily assisted up the bank by Standard No. 75074. With both locomotives working their hardest up the incline peaking at 1 in 50 you had to be there to hear, and see, the resulting cacophony of sound echoing firstly over the villages of Radipole and Upwey then in the cuttings leading into the two tunnels at the top. Within a month this would all be gone and only memories left. The volume of smoke emitted would these days be considered environmentally unfriendly but back then it was, to us enthusiasts, sheer nectar. The work put in, particularly by the fireman, in coaxing the often worn out badly maintained steam locomotives to please the masters in HQ and maintain schedules was probably never appreciated. Staying in a cottage at Upwey, halfway up the bank, many years later bought it all back to me – the replacement electric units seemingly not noticing the gradient.

The last Dorset terminus to mention is Bridport situated at the end of a 9½-mile branch line from Maiden Newton on the Yeovil to Weymouth. The original terminus of the branch, West Bay (née Bridport Harbour) was closed to passengers in 1930 and all services subsequently terminated at the town station. Always resourced from Weymouth depot it was a GWR/WR branch through and through – originally being constructed with the broad gauge track of 7ft ½in. Initially escaping the Beeching axe, the branch finally succumbed to closure as late as May 1975 – my only visit being on 'The Bridport Belle Rail Tour' of January 1967. Had the branch continued for just a few more years, I am certain that it would have qualified for a community grant from the local authority – thus ensuring its survival.

16

ROUTE TO THE 'STRONG' COUNTRY

We now return to the north-east of the Wessex region and take the ex-L&SWR route to Exeter, which diverges at Worting Junction – just 2½ miles west of Basingstoke. 'You're approaching the STRONG COUNTRY' said billboards, strategically placed in fields and lineside along this route, promising good beer for the thousands of holidaymakers heading west – the Romsey-based brewery having, in those pre-monopolistic days, a stranglehold of alcoholic outlets adjoining the line. Opened in its entirety in 1860 to compete with the GWR route to the West Country, the 130 miles from Basingstoke to Exeter was double-tracked throughout. When the Western Region took over the line in 1963 west of Salisbury it was always going to be rationalised in preference to 'their' route to the West Country and the myriad of intermediate halts and stations en route, together with the branch lines radiating from it, were swiftly disposed of. September 1964 was a pivotal month for it was then that the fast through-services to Devon and Cornwall, including the famed 'Atlantic Coast Express' were withdrawn. The substitute diesel-operated ('Warship') semi-fast services were a poor replacement, in respect of both reliability and performance, and as passengers drifted away the reduced train services led to large sections of the route being singled. It is only in recent years the short-sightedness of such a move is being rectified – believe it or not due to increased passenger numbers who are not prepared to suffer long delays on the alternative road network.

Salisbury, 83 miles from London, was the axis of the line and where either a change of crew or locomotive or a water stop took place (the SR system not being provided with troughs) meaning that all trains stopped there. An odd exception to this was the prestigious 'Devon Belle' that changed locomotives at Wilton a few miles west – in an attempt to reduce congestion at Salisbury. From September 1964 steam power west of Salisbury was only either on specials, diesel replacement owing to failures or the occasional local to Yeovil. The Salisbury shedmaster was fortunate in having a full complement of staff – not only was he able to 'loan' crews to other sheds when required, he also utilised them to clean his quota of 'Iron Horses'. You could often therefore tell a Salisbury-allocated locomotive from some distance away – they being the cleanest on the division. When he was transferred to Eastleigh, not being so flush with manpower, he offered overtime on Sundays to all grades to maintain an acceptable external appearance of the diminishing steam fleet. Needless to say the take-up was swiftly accepted and the 70D-allocated

With thanks to the Mid Hants Railway this replica Strong Country sign is on display at Alton.

Bournemouth-allocated West Country 4–6–2 No. 34040 *Crewkerne* comes off the spur at Reading West with the southbound 'The Pines Express' on 7 August 1964. This service had been deliberately diverted away from the S&D in September 1962 as a prelude to the usual 'closure by stealth' method often implemented by the authorities during the 1960s.

locomotives benefited accordingly – rivalling his ex-shed's examples. Name and numberplates were, towards the end, removed from the remaining locomotives, no doubt to thwart the possible profits reaped by potential souvenir-hunters – with only the support fixtures remaining it was as if the locomotive had already been condemned and stripped ready for embalming at their death. Replica name and numberplates were manufactured out of soup can lids and redundant carriage destination boards for fourteen 'selected' locomotives – the originals being placed in storage to evade souvenir-hunters. The genuine articles these days are worth a considerable amount of money as witnessed at specialist auction houses around the country.

Apart from passing through during three trips in 1964 it wasn't until the spring of 1965 that I began visiting the cathedral city of Salisbury more frequently. Only venturing away from the station to the nearest watering hole when the gaps in steam services became longer, the delights of the city were not chanced upon until much later in life. For several Saturdays that spring I stuck to a rigid plan (see below) which involved travelling on the 09.54 from Waterloo to Basingstoke, the northbound 'The Pines Express' to Banbury then returning on the daily York/Poole as far as Basingstoke – essentially to obtain runs with the fast-disappearing ex-GWR-powered services north of Oxford. Upon arrival back at Basingstoke I then caught the 16.48 all stations service to Salisbury, returning to London on what was to become infamous in respect of high speeds on the racing track east of Basingstoke, the lightweight 18.35. The 16.48 was an easily scheduled train which had sufficient time built in it for the detachment and attachment of vans at the midway point of the journey – Andover Junction. This perhaps was the sole surviving example of the many similar services, which used to operate, seemingly taking forever and a day from end to end, along the length of the L&SWR route to Exeter.

Time arr – dep	Station	27 March Traction	3 April Traction	24 April Traction	Miles
09.54	Waterloo	34026	34026	34005	
11.14 – 11.42	Basingstoke	35011	35023	34047	47¾
*	Oxford	D1711	D1685	D1701	41¾
13.25 – 14.33	Banbury	6848	6903	6990	22¾
	Oxford	34097	34036	34009	22¾
16.30 – 16.48	Basingstoke	34057	34057	34048	41¾
18.00 – 18.35	Salisbury	34089	34089	34052	36
20.21	Waterloo				83¾

* 'The Pines Express'
Mileage = 296½ miles

Further visits were made to Salisbury that spring to cover the soon-to-be dieselised Portsmouth to Cardiff services and as if to quantify steam's inexorable disappearance by that July, en route to the S&D I arrived at 02.39 behind a WR diesel (D7054) – before going forward down the main line with yet another WR diesel (D806) an hour later. The following year, with the decreasing number of steam trains available to us Waterloo commuters, depending on what engines were in circulation each night some of us often travelled down to Andover on this 17.00 Waterloo (albeit with a diesel) specifically to board the returning 18.35 ex-Salisbury from there. This service, worked by homegoing men to Basingstoke was the one which often produced some extremely fast times en route. Stories of that train's exploits during steam's swansong are legend – let's just say I was there when it mattered! The best run I recorded west of Basingstoke was on 26 September 1966 when Salisbury's No. 34013 *Okehampton* was working the five-coach, two-van train with Driver De'Ath of Basingstoke in charge. Ten miles out of Salisbury she topped the climb to milepost 73¼ at a creditable 64mph – attaining 94mph down Grateley bank before coming to a stand at Andover in 20 minutes 15 seconds (17½ miles). Another exhilarating start was made with Overton being passed at 83½mph, a max of 90mph being achieved along the slightly rising 1 in 350 before passing Oakley at 88mph – to be disappointingly delayed by adverse signals approaching both Worting Junction and Basingstoke – arriving there in 20 minutes 50 seconds (18½ miles). The motive power for the 18.35 ex-Salisbury was, unless 'guidance' from HQ was given, whatever Salisbury didn't want! As if to emphasise that point, on 12 April 1966 Standard 4MT No. 75069, having arrived a mere forty minutes previously, was turned round for the 18.35 departure. Any

What is this photograph taken at Banbury doing in a Southern Region-orientated book? In spring 1965, on three occasions I travelled there to sample ex-GWR power over the 22¾-mile route to Oxford on the 10.08 York to Poole service. Although 4–6–0 No. 6917 *Oldlands Hall* is the centerpiece of this 27 March 1965 shot, on the right in the bay is Worcester's No. 6848 *Toddington Grange* waiting to take over from the Type 3 (latterly Class 37) diesel which will have brought the train down the ex-GC route from the north. She would give way to SR power, usually a Bulleid Light Pacific, at Oxford.

West Country No. 34001 *Exeter* departs Oxford (from where she had taken the train over) on 28 August 1965 with the 08.35 Leeds City to Poole.

class of tender steam locomotive was liable to turn up on the train. Because of its light loading a 76xxx was sometimes used – struggling, however, to maintain the schedule. At Andover, the remaining stub of the cross-country route to Swindon, that of a freight branch to Ludgershall, was visited by myself (by road) as part of my wagon auditing duties – having to wait until 1986 when ex-GWR 4–6–0 No. 4930 *Hagley Hall* was working an open day shuttle service to cover the track by rail.

Perhaps just a brief synopsis of the route west of Salisbury, travelled over during 1964 and only afterwards on railtours, is appropriate. This wonderfully engineered line through the scenic Wiltshire and Devon countryside featured many switchback gradients as it crossed several river valleys. Deliberately constructing the line on the most direct, fastest route to the west with few speed restrictions, in order to compete and cream off the lucrative passenger traffic from the GWR, the nineteenth-century engineers certainly achieved their objective. This, however, meant that many sizeable towns, the best example being Shaftesbury, were not rail connected perhaps contributing to the poor patronage of the stations situated well away from the towns they purported to serve – resulting in their eventual downfall. Many of these 'wayside halts' closed during the early 1960s but, upon taking over in 1963, the Western Region ensured that this fine route was relegated to that of a secondary nature.

17

'THE KENNY BELLE'

The nickname 'The Kenny Belle' was given to the unadvertised passenger service operated between Clapham Junction and Kensington (Olympia) – run for the benefit of the then large workforce employed at the nearby Post Office Savings Bank HQ. Not surprisingly it was used by a great many other members of the public – the need for such a service requirement being vindicated by today's present-day operators providing a regular all-day interval service over the same tracks. Back in the 1960s, however, one set of four vehicles, which included the unique fibreglass-bodied BR Mk 1 suburban coach S1000S, which had seen service on both the Lancing Works staff train and Hayling Island services and has subsequently been preserved at the East Somerset Railway, was deemed sufficient. Departures from Clapham Junction were 08.16 and 08.46 (EWD), returning from Kensington at 08.33 (SX), 12.36 (SO), 16.36 (MTX), 17.06 (SX) or 17.36 (MTO) – all services allocated to be worked by a Nine Elms 4MT tank locomotive. The first train on a Monday morning (or the Tuesday after a Bank Holiday) and the last return on a Saturday used platform 1 (Windsor side) at Clapham Junction as the stock was berthed over the weekend in Clapham Yard. All other services departed from the Brighton side platform 17 which, if intending passengers for the train had forgotten these platform variations, would have had a herculean task in crowd avoidance in attempting to catch it – racing the length of the connecting footbridge spanning the carriage sidings.

An added complexity to beguile any non-GPO employee were days such as Maundy Thursday and Christmas Eve which were treated as Saturdays and as such the returning train ran to a lunchtime schedule. Aware of this arrangement, having studied the relevant railway publications, my first trip on the service was on the Thursday before Easter in 1965 when Standard 3MT 2–6–2T No. 82023 worked the 12.36 departure. To get to Kensington (Olympia) for a southbound steam departure involved ascertaining if an exhibition (such as the Ideal Home Exhibition) was being held in the nearby halls for which London Transport conveniently provided a District Line shuttle service from Earls Court – the alternative being a walk from Kensington High Street. An easier method was eventually achieved, having firstly acquired the authority from the guard, by boarding the outward empty stock working from Clapham Junction. Although never having come across any problems having showed some railway documentation to prove I was a railway employee, it was still a necessary act because had there been a mishap en route the guard would have been admonished in allowing a 'passenger' to travel on what was essentially a non-passenger train! Indeed similar showing of railway employment documentation often gained me access to all sorts of establishments

NINE ELMS DUTY NO. 106
4 MTT (STANDARD)
MONDAYS ONLY
OFF NO. 106 (SUNDAY)
    Waterloo
  c. Shunting 00 00 to 04 05
    Waterloo   04 50E
MONDAYS EXCEPTED
    C. Shunting 00 00 - 04 45
    ·Waterloo   04 50E

DAILY		
05 00		05 30
05 45	Clapham Jn	07 15
07 39	Nine Elms Loco	08 16P
08 24	Clap Jn (C)	08 33
08 41	Kensington (O)	08 46P
08 54	Clapham Jn (C)	09 00E
09 08	Kensington (O)	09 55
10 10	Clap Jn (W)	17 30
17 45	Nine Elms Loco	
	Waterloo	

    c. Shunting 17 45 to 24 00
    Work No. 106

NINE ELMS MEN
(1) Off No. 106 (SUN), work and rlvd in depot,
(2) 1st set on duty 05 25, relieve in depot, perform requirements, work, dispose and as ordered.
(3) 2nd set on duty 14 45, dispose No. 102, prepare and work this duty 17 30 and rlvd at Waterloo 21 15.
(4) 3rd set on duty 21 45, relieve at Waterloo 22 15, work and (MSX) relieved in depot (SO) relieved at Waterloo 06 15.

Locomotive and crew diagrams for 'The Kenny Belle'.

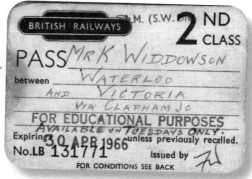

My 'free' route to Clapham Junction – thus enabling me to sample this unadvertised service prior to my rules and signalling classes.

Nine Elms' BR 3MT No. 82019 at Clapham Junction (platform 17 – Central side) on 16 February 1966 with the 08.16 for Kensington Olympia. Note the futuristic fibreglass single compartment vehicle in the formation.

BR 3MT No. 82019 again, I was to accumulate 114 miles with her crossing Chelsea Bridge on thirty-five occasions. Here she is at Kensington Olympia on 3 May 1966 with the 17.36 for Clapham Junction.

Ex-Exmouth Junction, now Nine Elms, BR 3MT No. 82018 departs Clapham Junction (platform 1 – Windsor side) on 7 February 1966 with the 08.16 for Kensington Olympia. The unique West London Junction signal-box spanning the tracks had had its steel roof removed the previous May – the weight (and rust!) contributing to the box subsiding.

or unorthodox travelling arrangements Joe Public would never have been allowed to embark upon – the reasoning being that as a railway employee you should have always been familiar with the rule book contents in event of any mishaps en route.

Being perhaps more interested in capturing runs behind Bulleids on the main line I only travelled on the 17.06 or 17.36 services on a mere twelve occasions during 1966, often catching runs with tank engines already travelled with having been displaced from their previous allocations – particularly Redhill and Templecombe. On a Tuesday evening this service neatly presented me at Clapham Junction in time for my Rules and Signalling evening class, a course recommended by the careers section, held in a room above the platforms – a side benefit of attendance being visits to Waterloo and Wimbledon 'A' signal-boxes.

Having left Waterloo in early 1966 on promotion within the clerical grades to be a 'journal marker' at DMO (SED) at Queen Street, a further move, this time to the Special Traffic section at DMO (SWD) at Wimbledon, beckoned just 9 months later. This latter move meant that the journey from my Kent home to Wimbledon involved travelling via Victoria with another change at Clapham Junction and if and when services were running to time it meant that at Clapham Junction I was able to catch the 08.16 out and 08.33 return en route to work. I was therefore able to say that even though I lived in steam-starved Kent I too, like several of my work colleagues who travelled in from Farnborough and Woking, commuted to work on steam trains! Although the morning service, for the final few months, was booked for a Standard 4MT Tank, any locomotive (i.e. Ivatt 2MT or Standard 3MT) available was provided. In total I made sixty-two journeys on 'The Kenny Belle' with sixteen different tank engines – accumulating 114 miles with the most common, No. 82019. Being unable to record the outward runs from Clapham because the train was so crowded (it was six a side in the single compartments) it was only resulting from myself usually being the only passenger on the returning 08.33 service that I was able to document runs with drivers synonymous with main line exploits on the somewhat more mundane route though the West London suburbs.

There were many speed restrictions along the 3¼-mile route – the fastest time overall time I recorded was 7 minutes 1 second with a max of 47mph between 'Pigeon Shit Bridge' (Hither Green drivers' nickname for the Thames crossing bridge which, in their opinion, was only held together by the said excrement) and Latchmere Junction. The highest speed I recorded was 51mph at West Brompton after an exhilarating departure from Olympia. Another bonus was the often sighting of one of London Transport's ex-GWR pannier locomotives at work in the Lille Bridge area. After steam finished, the service was worked by a Class 33 – crewed during various periods from Waterloo, Hither Green or Norwood depots. I made one final trip on the service and that was on Friday 1 October 1982 when Type 3 diesel 33208 with a Norwood crew worked the last loco-operated service. After that date Redhill-crewed DMMUs took over.

18

SPEED(Y) MERCHANTS

Over the years there have been many other authors more knowledgeable than I who have written articles detailing SR steam locomotive performances, the power ratio, output, coal usage in relation to speed, etc. I do not profess to know the ins and outs of why this happened or that occurred – all I remember (helped by extensive notes taking at the time) is that it was a privilege to have witnessed and participated in the wonderful finale of Bulleid's Pacifics during the last few months of the Iron Horses' reign on the Waterloo services.

Several steam drivers adopted a gung-ho attitude, obtaining previously unheard of speeds over the well-fettled permanent way formation theoretically provided for the new electrics. With most permanent way speed restrictions lifted, the newly relaid track was an inevitable lure for certain drivers to push their machines to their limit. Taking into consideration that they were destined for the scrap yard in the not-too-distant future, any failure or defect caused by excessive speed would be attributed to the hapless locomotives' poor, run-down condition. While some signalmen sometimes reported fast running (i.e. by breaking the 85mph maximum steam traction was officially allowed) management seemingly turned a blind eye to such occasions preferring to promote the new clean image that the eventual inauguration of the brand new electrics would provide (albeit three months later than originally anticipated!).

It was impossible to be aboard all the attempted 100mph runs but word of mouth usually ensured that most were known about – the drivers themselves tipping us off as regards which train or turn they were working. If, however, a poor-performing Bulleid or any Standard 5MT was allocated to the designated train, taking into consideration the driver was unlikely to be able to perform miracles we looked elsewhere to chase our particular favourites or other wants or needs. While the acceleration and sound of them was sometimes spectacular, the fastest speed I ever recorded with a Standard 5 was a mere 82mph. I was lucky enough to eventually obtain thirty instances of speeds over 90mph (see p. 129) of which four attained the magic 100mph – with 'Merchant Navy' No. 35003 *Royal Mail* perhaps being the most prolific performer, certainly since Salisbury shed 'adopted' her, and shook off her nickname 'Royal Snail' with some unbelievable runs. One particular evening, just two weeks before the end, I boarded the 18.15 semi-fast Weymouth to Waterloo at Basingstoke not realising another never-to-be-repeated experience was about to be enacted. Working the train was Nine Elms Driver Burridge and

8P No. 35008 *Orient Line* pauses at Southampton Central on 11 February 1966 while working the 13.25 Weymouth to Waterloo. In September 1966 I chased her for three days accumulating 629½ miles, thus contributing to an eventual 1,450 miles.

An unusually clean 'Merchant Navy' No. 35013 *Blue Funnel* at Southampton Central on 5 February 1967 with the 11.30 Waterloo to Weymouth. At a mere 541 miles (after that journey) there were obviously a few more trips with her to result in an eventual 1,748!

The 'main man', Gordon Porter, storming up the bank at Basingstoke. Although a Nine Elms driver he resided at Basingstoke and commuted from there.

the speed machine herself – a lethal combination! The well-documented maximum of 106mph (between mileposts 38 and 39) has subsequently been acknowledged as the highest steam speed recorded on SR metals. As regards the attempted ton speeds I can only assume the firemen who worked with such drivers were fully compliant to fuel the increased workload required – not for them was the need to visit any gym to induce Olympian muscles!

I will never forget the exhilarating feeling of anticipation, when crossing Battledown flyover, having stormed up Winchester bank, being put over to the through-line at Worting Junction sighting a clear road, for possible high speeds ahead. The combination of an enthusiastic driver and a Bulleid in fine form was a lethal mix, which can never be recreated on today's railway system. The leading coach of these trains was not necessarily the best place for 'normal' members of the public. With all available windows open and occupied by enthusiasts looking for mileposts in order to record speeds on our stopwatches and in our notebooks, the inevitable coal dust, cinders and smoke poured in. Any attempt to concentrate enough to read a paper or book surely must have been abandoned by the sometimes-alarming hunting the coach took on at high speed! I do remember we frequently used Optrex by the bathful upon reaching home in an attempt to wash out grit trapped under our eyelids. To this day, even though I write right-handed, I still wear my wristwatch on that hand – the left being in use operating a stopwatch.

Loco	Driver	Date	Train	Load	Speed	Location
34001	Porter/70A	04/07/67	02.45 Wloo/Bomo	3c3v	92	MP31-Hook
					98	Winchester Jct
34009	Cumming/70A	16/06/66	18.38 Salis/Wloo	4c5v	93	Fleet
34013	De'Ath/Basing	26/09/66	18.38 Salis/Wloo	5c2v	94	Grateley/Red Post
					90	Oakley/Overton
34015	Gray/70A	15/03/67	18.38 Salis/Wloo	5c2v	90	B'wood/Woking
34021	Porter/70A	05/02/67	18.03 Bomo/Wloo	10c	90	Fleet/Fb'oro
34036	Porter/70A	19/01/67	17.30 Wey/Wloo	9c2v	90	Winchfield/Fleet
					90	Fleet/Fb'oro
34037	Davies/70A	05/05/67	18.38 Salis/Wloo	5c2v	97	Winchfield/Fleet
34047	Sloper/70D	27/12/66	22.30 Wloo/Bomo	7c	90	Wootton/Wallers A
34095	Porter/70A	08/07/67	02.45 Wloo/Bomo	3c 5v	90	Fleet/Winchfield
				3c 4v	94	Wootton/Wallers A
34098	Porter/70A	17/01/67	17.30 Wey/Wloo	9c2v	95	Woking Jct
					93	Woking
					95	West Byfleet
					90	Weybridge/Hersham

Loco	Driver	Date	Train	Load	Speed	Location
34102	Groome/70A	21/04/67	18.38 Salis/Wloo	5c1v	98	Fleet
35003	Enticnap/70A	19/04/67	18.38 Salis/Wloo	5c1v	100	Winchfield/Fleet
35003	Groome/70A	20/04/67	18.38 Salis/Wloo	6c1v	98	Fleet
					90	F'boro
					93	MP31/B'wood
35003	Hendicott/70A	23/04/67	11.30 Wloo/Wey	6c1v	95	Wallers A/W'chester
35003	Chapman/70A	27/04/67	18.38 Salis/Wloo	6c1v	101	Winchfield/Fleet
					100	Fleet/F'boro
					100	B'wood
35003	Matthews/70A	04/05/67	18.38 Salis/Wloo	8c2v	90	Fleet/F'boro
35003	Burridge/70A	26/06/67	18.15 Wey/Wloo	3c2v	106	Winchfield/Fleet
					101	Fleet/F'boro
35007	Domm/70A	06/07/67	17.30 Wey/Wloo	10c	98	Fleet/F'boro
35012	Parsons/70A	07/04/67	08.35 Wloo/Wey	8c2v	94	Winchester Jct
35013	Porter/70A	18/01/67	17.30 Wey/Wloo	9c2v	93	Winchfield/Fleet
35016		22/05/64	18.20 Bomo/Wloo	12c1v	91	Winchfield/Fleet
35023	West/70A	13/09/66	18.38 Salis/Wloo	5c5v	90	Fleet
					92	B'wood
35023	Hooker/70A	15/10/66	Rail Tour	8c	101	Hbourne/Andover
35023	Kelly/70A	15/10/66	Rail Tour	8c	90	Grateley/Red Post
						B'wood/Woking
35023	Rickman/70A	18/05/67	18.38 Salis/Wloo	8c2v	92	Fleet
					94	B'wood/Woking
35028	Porter/70A	16/12/66	17.30 Wey/Wloo	11c1v	91	Basing/Hook
					94	Winchfield/Fleet
35028	Dent/70A	19/06/67	17.30 Wey/Wloo	10c1v	90	Winchfield/Fleet
					91	Fleet/F'boro
35028	West/70A	25/04/67	08.35 Wloo/Wey	8c1v	94	Wallers A/W'chester
35030	Sloper/70D	04/02/67	17.30 Wey/Wloo	9c2v	97	Winchfield/Fleet

70A – Nine Elms
70D – Eastleigh
Note – a highly recommendable website for 70A staff reminiscences is: http://svsfilm/nineelms/

19

OUT OF COURSE RUNNING

Looking back through my tattered notebooks while researching for this book, every now and then I came across an item, noted at the time of being a bit different, that brought all the wonderful memories flooding back. Just about every evening during that last year I, together with many others, travelled from Waterloo on services we knew one day would finish. We were recording history – so every little 'happening' was worth noting. Why and what to do with it were questions that were too far away. Perhaps one day we might document it so that people who had never experienced a steam-operated rush hour could read about it. So this final chapter begins with a series of 'oddities' – occurrences that don't sit neatly elsewhere. They are a reflection of those times and detail individual instances, which made travelling behind steam during that period so memorable. Here goes then.

The 17.30 Waterloo to Bournemouth was an express steam departure at the height of the rush hour and any late departures severely impacted upon the intensive electric services. It was dieselised in October 1966 but due to their high failure rate (sometimes causing delayed starts while suitable replacement power was found), was returned to steam five weeks later, only to be redieselised after another five weeks, again eventually being turned over to the inevitable REP/TCs in March 1967. Twice when I was aboard, the train was stopped additionally at Woking, which, from a selfish point of view, was beneficial in allowing me to alight and pursue further catches that night. Severe icing to the third rail one January night decimated the EMU service and the 17.30 was used as a suburban relief service – the other occasion was when the signalman stopped it there because the locomotive's electric headlights were not working, a seven-minute station stop being made while oil replacements were located. A different reason for delay at Waterloo one August evening amounted to 54 seconds when Driver Hadley, having started away, then stopped, jumped off the footplate and rescued his cap from the platform.

The 17.09 Waterloo to Basingstoke also caused rush hour dislocation if delayed and on one occasion one of my more eccentric colleagues, Stewpot, was himself late in leaving our Wimbledon office and, unlikely to get to Waterloo in time for the train, somehow arranged for a special stop order to be issued for it to call additionally at Wimbledon. When the guard exclaimed that he had no idea why he had to stop, Stewpot was quoted as saying 'because I wanted it to' – for which I believe he was unsurprisingly disciplined! Still with the 17.09 service and an eleven-minute delay at Woking was collected one day when *Okehampton* had to set back twice before obtaining clean rail to restart the train – water, grease and oil always being associated with regular stopping points at stations. I stood on the platform in awe, watching the skill of the crew struggling with the situation. I was to learn then that Bulleid's Pacifics were always prone to slipping upon starting and eventually, with increasing confidence, *Okehampton* began to accelerate away emitting the uniquely recognisable sounds that will always be associated with them before disappearing into the distance. Two and a half years later and Woking was the scene of much complaining from bowler-hatted gentlemen after Standard Mogul No. 76064, the Nine Elms foreman obviously short of anything stronger, was turned out for the eleven-coach 18.09 service. Having taken nearly forty-seven minutes to arrive there (with a max of 50mph through Surbiton), she sat awaiting the requisite boiler pressure, finally departing twenty-two minutes late.

Away from the rush hour but involving sister No. 76058, an eventful journey on the Down Mails (22.35 ex-Waterloo) in April 1967 was encountered. Having struggled from the start with the ten-vehicle train, Driver Sloper stopped at Surbiton for ten minutes to regain boiler pressure eventually reaching Woking in fifty-four minutes, with a max of 48mph en route. A replacement locomotive, in the form of No. 73018, took the Mails away seventy minutes late. Woking again and in February 1965, having heard through the grapevine (the only reliable method of communication in those far off pre-mobile days) that No. 34051 *Winston Churchill* was working an Up Semi three days after her funeral duties, I negotiated a long lunch time and travelled down for her. I had several copies of my photograph printed for sale to NON-enthusiasts – she had been on TV after all!

Engineering notices were always studied carefully during this period and steam diversions over unusual routes were homed in on. In November 1965 Merchant No. 26 took me via the Byfleet/Addlestone curve and Twickenham and a double helping of diversions in June 1966, firstly with *Yeovil* on the 03.15 Papers via the Guildford New Line and Pompey Direct (with me being the only passenger on the three-coach two-van train) and secondly by doubling back to Woking for *Whimple* (alas with diesel assistance) over 'The Alps'. The slack timings allowed for services in the run-up to electrification was proven one Sunday morning when the 11.30 from Waterloo not only stopped at Roundwood signal-box to offload coal before reversing at Micheldever over to the Up line (SLW in operation), but *still* managing to arrive into Bournemouth eleven minutes early. On another Sunday, while on the 09.33 excursion from Waterloo, an engineer's jack was run over – appearing through the floor on our compartment!

Now to the 15.50 from Weymouth – a somewhat slow semi which if one had been bashing all day in Hampshire was prone to being slept on throughout my journey back to the smoke. An excessively slow seventy-six minutes between Basingstoke and Woking (23 miles) was awarded me behind *Salisbury* one August evening – the cause being a complete failure of the pneumatic signalling system. On another occasion *Sir Eustace* (sometimes misheard as useless) *Missenden* arrived at Basingstoke forty minutes late, then stood a further forty minutes at the platform. The delay was attributable to defective brakes and we eventually departed with 16½in of vacuum – 21 being the norm. This didn't hinder the driver who then obtained a maximum of 79mph through Esher – would the train have been allowed to proceed in today's safety-conscious world?

Having failed to restart the 17.09 Waterloo to Basingstoke from the normal stopping point adjacent to Woking signal-box, West Country No. 34013 *Okehampton* had to reverse onto clean rail thus enabling me to obtain this shot on 7 October 1964.

Included within this book as the only respectable shot of an ex-LSWR 4–6–0 S15 locomotive No. 30837 is captured arriving at Woking on 19 May 1965 with the 19.02 Parcels Waterloo to Southampton Terminus.

7P5F Unmodified Pacific No. 34051 *Winston Churchill* three days after her funeral duties at Woking while working the 11.00 Bournemouth West to Waterloo. The grapevine had activated as to her working the train and my manager had allowed me to travel to Woking in my (extended) lunchtime to catch a run with her. I had many prints of this photograph made for numerous non-enthusiasts requesting copies!

The Banbury-allocated Black 5, which laid over at Bournemouth in between the Saturday and Monday York services, was often used on London services. Being a Tuesday (21 June 1966) it was most surprising to see No. 45349 on the 15.50 service. While 'new' for a number of my colleagues, I had already travelled with the Tyseley-allocated locomotive over ex-GC metals and was not as happy as them!

My travels as documented are obviously from the public side of the railways, the enjoyment achieved being in a relatively clean and comfortable environment. For the train crews it was a different matter. The irregular and unsocial hours amid filthy conditions, both at sheds and on footplates, working with unkempt and unreliable steam locomotives, must have been a nightmare. When booking on, I have no doubt that the duties and trains they worked sometimes bore little resemblance to what their rostered duties should have been. The backbreaking and often monotonous nature of locomotive preparations must have been a major disincentive to many and the 1960s period of full employment led to obvious staff shortages – in turn causing extra tasks for top link drivers who had expected their steeds to have been fully prepared for them. Was it any wonder that both the Southern Region management, together with a great many employees, looked forward to the cleaner environment that electrification brought them? However, when steam traction ceased some footplate staff found that the 'magic' of the job had disappeared and finding it difficult to adjust, left the railway service to pursue a different career – perhaps sating their previous desires as volunteers on what is now, but not known in 1967, a burgeoning preserved railway scene.

20

THE FINAL WEEK: JULY 1967

S aturday 1 July 1967 dawned bright and sunny but, for Southern steam followers, the clouds were gathering on the horizon. A mere eight days hence, the inevitable cessation of London's last steam trains was to take place. We, a disparate collection of like-minded individuals who over the previous few years had 'commuted' most evenings on Waterloo's steam services, knew that the electrification of the Bournemouth line deferred twice before would finally be implemented at 00.01 on Monday 10 July 1967. With so few services booked for steam operation at weekends, coupled with the fact that I had only accrued a mere nine instances of steam travel during the previous five days, in a bid to avoid full-on depression I reasoned that a trip to Carlisle was likely to be more rewarding. With fingers crossed, nothing being guaranteed, the first running of the Summer Saturday-only 13.20 Euston to Glasgow was boarded. While it was a steam turn between Crewe and Carlisle during the summer of 1966 the inexorable tide of dieselisation was forever encroaching on many former guaranteed steam services, so it was with an immense sense of relief that the recognisable outline of a Britannia tender hoved into view from her 'hiding' position around the corner on the Chester lines at Crewe. A glorious non-stop daytime 141-mile run over Shap with No. 70025 *Western Star* made the journey north well worthwhile. All booked services returning south were diesel-operated, but a previous perusal of the Special Traffic Notice had revealed an Inverness to Euston relief train departing at 02.15 hours on the Sunday morning. The long wait paid dividends when a 'required' Kingmoor-allocated Black 5 No. 44727 arrived in the centre road just after 02.00 a.m. The ever-increasingly nocturnal aspects of our hobby was surely tested that morning because resulting from the train's late running, eventual departure being 02.58, a lot of 'stay awake stamina' was required! Taking periodic perambulations around the station away from the sleep-inducing warm coal-fired waiting room, upon the train's arrival I luckily found an empty compartment – falling asleep to the sound of the Blackie battling up the gradients of Shap Fell. With an arrival into Euston at 09.05 I might just have made the 09.33 excursion out of Waterloo (No. 34025) but, with three further overnights planned during the coming week, I decided to go home and have an early night in a comfortable bed.

Steam bows out on the Mail services

By the final week the only booked steam departures out of Waterloo were as follows: the 02.30 to Portsmouth, 02.45 to Bournemouth, 04.40 and 07.18 to Salisbury, 08.10 and 08.35 to Weymouth, 17.23 (FO) to Bournemouth and the 18.54 to Salisbury. With such a large gap of departures during the day I surmised that the only method to obtain any respectable mileages was to forfeit several nights' sleep – well it WAS the LAST week! On Monday 3 July, after a full day's work at my Wimbledon office I caught 'The Pram', nickname for 'Merchant Navy' No. 35023, on that evening's 18.54 departure from Waterloo. Going on to Winchester I then travelled with Standard No. 73020 on the 21.18 (18.15 Weymouth) back up to Woking. The original plan was to stay on this train to Waterloo for the following morning's Paper train departures of 02.30 and 02.45. That day's 'Bournemouth Belle' had, however, arrived into Waterloo with Light Pacific No. 34025 *Whimple* rather than the booked Brush diesel and so, as always relying on the possibility rather than probability, I alighted at Woking in the hope that return working for the diesel, the 22.35 Mails Waterloo to Weymouth, might also be steam-operated. Fortune was on my side and *Whimple* had been serviced, coaled and watered during the five-hour turnaround and duly arrived into Woking at 23.22. What a result – not only was I to enjoy unexpected extra steam miles but also the bonus of a warm comfortable seat for the first two hours of the night. Study of my bible (the ever-present dog-eared working timetable) revealed a mere sixteen-minute wait at Southampton to connect into the opposite way working was possible, and as expected the 22.13 Up Mails Weymouth to Waterloo duly arrived into Southampton behind a diesel – albeit a few minutes late. Without knowing or caring about the reason why, D1926 was detached and sent scuttling off towards Eastleigh. There was a growing sense of anticipation as the minutes passed by while awaiting for replacement power to materialise through the inky darkness of the tunnel. A second stroke of good fortune in the form of 'Battle of Britain' No. 34087 *145 Squadron* was to take us forward and unaware of it at the time, this night was to see the LAST steam-operated Mail service in either direction – the diesels behaving themselves, on those trains at least, for the rest of the week. I had resigned myself, resulting from the late running, to missing the Down Papers services from Woking (03.11 and 03.29) but yet a third stroke of luck was to befall me. Standard No. 73020, booked for the 02.30, was failed at Nine Elms resulting in Light Pacific No. 34102 *Lapford*, booked for the 02.45, stepping up to cover. Sister Modified No. 34001 *Exeter* was turned out for the Bournemouth Papers and, luckily for me, was running six minutes late. The infamous Driver Porter had changed his shifts and was on the 02.45 for several days that week and on this Tuesday morning proceeded to attain 92mph near Hook and 98mph down Winchester bank – prior to stopping, with the smell of burning brake blocks, at Winchester City. What a great end to the night's travels.

Returning from Southampton I went to work, no doubt detailing my adventures to all who asked about my dishevelled appearance. Having completed the required hours I returned to Southampton that evening for an unmemorable performance behind *Whimple* (again!) on the 17.30 Weymouth to Waterloo (due 20.51) before heading home for some decent sleep.

Portsmouth and Bournemouth visits

On Wednesday 5 July, a further day's work was accomplished before travelling down via 'The Alps' to Southampton for the 17.30 ex-Weymouth – 19.14 departure. An even time run of 78 minutes 48 seconds (79¼ miles) was obtained with 'Merchant Navy' No. 35023 *Holland-Afrika Line* with a maximum of 87mph en route. Several hours were passed in the BRSA club and an all-night café at the nearby Waterloo Road before returning to the station for Thursday morning's 02.45 Bournemouth train. Driver Porter was again on it but he had Standard 5MT No. 73029 and although externally clean (and green!) he didn't expect 'anything spectacular'. Light Pacific No. 34036 *Westward Ho!* was on the 02.30 Portsmouth Harbour Papers and so, taking into consideration I needed a mere 107 miles to take me over 1,000 with her, I opted for that train – attaining the magic figure on the returning 07.30 Portsmouth and Southsea to Eastleigh train. Having already booked a day's annual leave I consulted the 'bible' to ascertain how to make the most of it. With careful planning, taking into consideration the few steam services available to travel on, I then went up to Basingstoke and caught 'Merchant Navy' No. 35008 on the 08.30 Waterloo to Weymouth, alighting at Bournemouth. With just an hour to wait, the 11.18 Weymouth to Waterloo, having been brought in by Mogul No. 76006, was taken over by 'Battle of Britain' No. 34087 for the 108-mile journey back to the capital. Has the reader noticed that no more than a dozen steam locomotives were circulating that week and time and time again I was coming across them? Any steam, however, was welcome – next week all would be gone.

The 15.35 semi back to Southampton was caught with Class 73 Electro-diesel E6049; it was on electric power so my diesel-devoid departures out of Waterloo still stood. This neatly connected into the 17.30 ex-Weymouth (boarded for the third occasion that week) rewarding me with an excellent run with Driver Domm (70A) – normally not known for exceeding the official 85mph maximum. The locomotive was No. 35007 *Aberdeen Commonwealth* and, having topped Roundwood at an astonishing 71mph, was all set for the magic ton when, passing Fleet (at 98mph), she suffered severe internal damage (hot big end or blown middle cylinder?). After being coaxed the 30 remaining miles to Waterloo, she was withdrawn from service upon arrival at Nine Elms – my personal mileage finishing up at 2,003. This train was one of the few non-stop Southampton to Waterloo expresses, which Nine Elms men worked and were often known to swap shifts to work it. Some months previously when the drivers' duties were different it was an Eastleigh turn and Driver Sloper, who was having a great run with No. 34098 *Templecombe,* had to terminate the train at Walton-on-Thames when a hot box on the tender developed.

Lord Dowding and 'The Pram' bow out

Friday 7 July dawned and having made my final trip to work on 'The Kenny Belle', that night saw me on the 17.23 Friday-only train – unusually formed of LMR maroon coaching stock. With a considerable number of enthusiasts aboard, indeed progressively during the week increasing numbers were being noted, an uninspiring run was had behind Modified Pacific No. 34093 *Saunton*. At Basingstoke the 19.06 to Eastleigh was sitting in the Down bay. This train used to be worked by the 17.09 ex-Waterloo locomotive after its arrival at 18.28, but since dieselisation of the London train the previous month, the provision of the power was random. A short, unusual and rarely photographed working, it was formed of three coaches and an assortment of vans. On that very last Friday I espied my favourite Light Pacific, No. 34052 *Lord Dowding*, on it and so I just had to travel with her one last time – subsequently alighting off of the Waterloo train at Winchester catching my final 7 miles with her. No other enthusiast was on board – was I the only one who cared for her? Over the final two days she worked overnight ballasts from Dorchester South to Wareham and onto Weymouth and I was able to 'acquire' the guard's journals for both the passenger and the final two trains she ever worked. Unable to continue with her beyond Eastleigh (she formed an all stations to Bournemouth service) I caught a diesel unit to Southampton in order to board the 20.42 (18.15 ex-Weymouth) to Waterloo – Light Pacific No. 34095 *Brentnor* performing the task without any heroics en route.

The numbers of enthusiasts were now swelling in size and from 23.00 to 02.00 outnumbered the resident vagrants awaiting the soup supply from the Salvation Army.

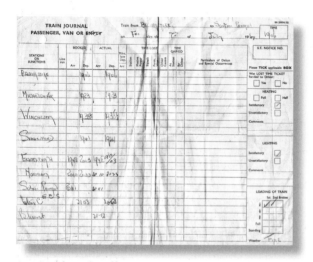

Acquired from the offices at my place at work was *Lord Dowding's* final passenger duty log.

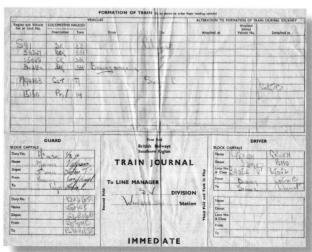

It was now Saturday 8 July and with none of us interested in watching the advent of colour TV that afternoon (the first ever transmission was of the Wimbledon tennis championships) we all were eagerly waiting to see what Driver Porter was going to bring up from Nine Elms on his last main line duty. Amazingly, a mere three hours after arrival, *Brentnor* was turned around for it – still, it was better than a Standard. Knowing, perhaps, that he was being watched, he asked us to keep a low profile prior to departure so we sat in the compartments quietly anticipating possible record-breaking achievements ahead – with just four 'normal' passengers and 129 enthusiasts it was like trying to keep a lid on a pot of boiling water! *Brentnor* managed to take 35 minutes to Woking, not helped by a signal stand at Hampton Court Junction and the preceding *Clovelly* on the 02.30 Portsmouth. A mere 87mph max was then attained between there and Basingstoke but then the fireworks started with ONLY 94mph being reached approaching Wallers Ash – the engine being described by Porter as 'sluggish' when we alighted at Southampton. With the tender 'dancing around' during the journey most of us in the front coach, which was suffering violent oscillations, had to duck from the lumps of flying coal some of which broke several windows. Later reports show 93mph was made approaching, and sliding past, Christchurch. That the steam engine is a living thing and requires a bit of TLC to fulfil its potential was proof that morning – as compared to her performance in April 1966 while working the 17.30 ex-Weymouth when she had to stop at Winchester Junction for eight minutes for a blow-up resulting in a loss of thirty minutes on an easily scheduled non-stop Southampton to Waterloo. A fair majority of us alighted at Southampton to return for the last booked Weymouth steam departure from Waterloo, the 08.30, deliberately diagrammed steam for the day. The 06.07 all stations diesel unit decided to suffer a temporary fault at Winchester thus missing the connection at Basingstoke for Waterloo. Many phone calls were made to the Control to try to stop the Weymouth service at Woking but unable to guarantee it, thirty or so of us, upon arrival at Basingstoke, caught the 07.35 to Salisbury (04.40 ex-Waterloo) with Mogul No. 76066 in charge and after just making a two-minute connection into a Portsmouth-bound diesel, we awaited the Weymouth service at Southampton – duly arriving with 'Merchant Navy' No. 35023 at the front. We found that it had indeed stopped additionally at Woking and so all parties, and indeed a great many more, were reunited. It had the atmosphere of a rail tour with photographers all along the line – in fields and up trees and among the deer and ponies of the New Forest. How I have often subsequently wished that I could have been in two places at once – I sadly scour the railway magazines these days and whenever espying a photograph of a train I was aboard extract it into my 'I was there' files!

Anyway back to that final Saturday and seemingly the entire enthusiast fraternity travelled all the way to the end of the line – arriving eight minutes late at 12.04. Knowing that she would return on the 15.55 ex-Weymouth Quay (from Weymouth Junction) to London later that day, a 'fill-in' trip to Wareham on the three-coach 12.12 all stations service with Standard No. 73092 was the order of the day. The train was packed to the gunwales with us enthusiasts – the locals looking on in amazement! After returning to Weymouth behind D6512, an example of the replacement diesel power to be used on all services west of Bournemouth the following week, a nearby café was besieged with orders – mostly involving chips. My notes show 'an unsuccessful attempt was made to board the returning boat train'. My memory fails me as to what exactly what happened but perhaps the fact that the boat train changed locomotives at a point adjacent to the shed – i.e. away from the town station – had something to do with it. We therefore all had to travel on the preceding 15.50 diesel-operated service train (D6538) to Poole where, while the public timetable showed the boat train as NOT stopping, we all knew it had to for a banking locomotive to be attached at the rear, as far as Bournemouth, to assist the lengthy train up the 1 in 60 Parkstone bank. No. 35023 duly arrived into Poole adorned with chalk-messaged graffiti all over her smokebox, the most predominant of which was 'THE END'. Again literally hundreds of people were out and about crowding the stations and tracksides to witness this historic event. The crew were inundated with requests for souvenir lumps of coal and autographs. It was a sad but memorable occasion with most people assuming that this was THE LAST steam train from Weymouth to Waterloo.

The very last steam train into London

It was now the VERY last day – Sunday 9 July. Having arrived at Waterloo and being prepared to pay the supplement enabling travel on the all-Pullman 'Bournemouth Belle' which had been specifically diagrammed for steam on the final day (by John – a DMO Wimbledon diagram clerk/enthusiast), the authorities, not wanting any publicity associated to glamourise the scenario, had rerostered a Brush diesel to the 12.30 departure and 16.37 return. A more knowledgeable diagram clerk than I (Mike) sat down and calculated that as a consequence of this rediagramming move, there would be no diesel available for the 14.07 Weymouth to Waterloo train. So, keeping our fingers crossed that the DEMU via 'The Alps' wouldn't fail similar to the previous day's debacle, we travelled out on the 12.27 via Alton service. Arriving with minutes to spare at Southampton, and being unaware of the will it or won't it work beyond Bournemouth scenario (the loco was initially detached upon arrival only to be reattached again), the wonderful sight and sound of 'Merchant Navy' No. 35030 *Elder Dempster Line* hoved into view. Although grateful to have made the connection and be part of the occasion, it was indeed a sad day for all us Southern enthusiasts. The atmosphere was less frenetic than the previous day perhaps because the provision of steam on this service was so unexpected. Quite a few people I knew stayed with their original plan of an out and back trip on the 'Belle', hoping for some divine intervention but alas not happening, for a return steam journey. After arriving at Waterloo ten minutes early (17.46), everyone hung around to see Driver Evans take her to Nine Elms – and that was it.

What now? For me personally I spent the remaining weekends that year 'Oop North'. Although some time was spent in the Manchester and Preston areas during 1968 prior to the elimination of BR steam that August, the majority of my time was spent chasing new catches in Europe.

Nowadays, when I look through the myriad of photographic albums of steam trains available in specialist bookshops I sometimes wonder why it had to be in my era (1960s) that the changes had to be made. For many years steam reigned supreme and nothing changed. Year after year the passage of branch line trains and main line expresses went on unaffected by world and local events. Scenes our parents took for granted would seemingly always be there – the 1960s however brought change and not always for the better. A great many railway infrastructure establishments i.e. stations, depots, tracks, etc. are now car parks, supermarkets and housing estates and I often wonder if any of the present-day users realise

The very last steam train into the capital. John Bird's photograph of the 14.07 Weymouth to Waterloo at Southampton Central on Sunday 9 July 1967 – with 'Merchant Navy' No. 35030 *Elder Dempster Lines.*

what hallowed ground they are standing on. Someone once said progress would be a wonderful thing if only it would stop. When steam finally disappeared from the Southern Region in July 1967 I had no cause to travel out of Waterloo any more until eighteen years later when my brother's bank moved from Cheshire to Poole, he following the job. This subsequently attracted my parents who retired to Bournemouth and having often visited the area as a result, I have many happy memories of the Wessex area – with the choice of busy coastal resorts or the tranquillity of the surrounding countryside to choose from. For me though, the excitement and camaraderie of those final years when friendly rivalry of mileage chasing was a greater part of my life, will never be forgotten. While researching through my tattered, worn notebooks for this book, a lot of happy memories were relived. For those who were part of that same scene, I hope so for you as well.

Time arr – dep	Station	Traction	Notes
*	Wimbledon	EMU	Mon 3 July
* – 18.54	Waterloo	35023	
20.17 – 20.23	Basingstoke	DEMU	
20.48 – 21.18	Winchester City	73020	
22.20 – 23.22	Woking	34025	
01.05 – 01.21	Southampton Central	34087	Tue 4 July
03.00 – 03.29	Woking	34001	
05.09 – 06.07	Southampton Central	DEMU	
06.56 – 07.14	Basingstoke	EMU	
08.22 – *	Waterloo	EMU	
* – 16.53	Wimbledon	EMU	
18.01 – 18.05	Alton	DEMU	
19.03 – 19.14	Southampton Central	34025	

Time arr – dep	Station	Traction	Notes
20.51	Waterloo		
16.53	Wimbledon	EMU	Wed 5 July
18.01 – 18.05	Alton	DEMU	
19.03 – 19.14	Southampton Central	35023	
20.51 – 02.30	Waterloo	34036	Thu 6 July
05.39 – 06.56	Portsmouth & Southsea	EMU	
07.02 – 07.33	Fratton	34036	
08.15 – 08.41	Eastleigh	DEMU	
09.19 – 09.48	Basingstoke	35008	
11.29 – 12.35	Bournemouth Central	34087	
14.52 – 15.35	Waterloo	E6049	
17.47 – 19.14	Southampton Central	35007	
20.51	Waterloo		
08.16	Clapham Junction	41319	Fri 7 July
08.24 – 08.33	Kensington Oval	41319	
08.41 – *	Clapham Junction	EMU	
* – *	Wimbledon	EMU	
* – 17.23	Waterloo	34093	
18.47 – 19.35	Winchester City	34052	
19.48 – 20.07	Eastleigh	DEMU	
20.21 – 20.42	Southampton Central	34095	
22.56 – 02.45	Waterloo	34095	Sat 8 July
05.09 – 06.07	Southampton Central	DEMU	
06.56 – 07.35	Basingstoke	76066	
08.40 – 08.42	Salisbury	DEMU	
09.18 –10.08	Southampton Central	35023	
11.56 –12.12	Weymouth	73092	
13.05 – 13.22	Wareham	D6512	
13.56 – 15.50	Weymouth	D6538	
16.44 – 17.00	Poole	35023	
19.49	Waterloo		
13.27	Waterloo	EMU	Sun 9 July
14.47 – 14.53	Alton	DEMU	
15.46 – 16.13	Southampton Central	35030	
17.56	Waterloo		

* times not noted

AN AFTERTHOUGHT

Fast forward to 2011 and when writing this 'afterthought' I am visiting Somerset once more – you may recall the introduction was also penned in this wonderful county two years earlier. Now it's just the two of us, my daughter preferring Lanzarote to Exmoor, and while relaxing in the garden of a self-catering barn at a farm near Crowcombe the stillness of the afternoon was broken only by the 'oohs' and 'ahhs' of the ritual Andy Murray defeat at Wimbledon on a nearby TV. But wait what else can I hear? Why it's the chime whistle of the 'new' build A2 No. 60163 *Tornado* on the nearby West Somerset Railway. Visiting the WSR after a lengthy boiler refit in Germany, when booking this break in February I had no inkling that the surprise catch of Britain's newest steam locomotive was on the cards. Steam catches back in the 1960s were often by chance – nowadays with the internet and planned outings for steam locomotives, only a late failure or replacement causes the long-forgotten surprise element of our hobby. So I've still got the steam bug. Although never travelling overnight (the comfort of a bed each night perhaps reflecting the ageing bones' needs) I still 'guide' my wife to visit some of the many preserved railways where the likelihood of a new catch is in the offing. Who would have thought, in 1968, that hundreds of wrecks would be restored to operational status by bands of dedicated enthusiasts, thus allowing like-minded 'chasers' to continue their personal pursuits? Perhaps one day I might have caught them all – but with (currently) many still 'required' the flame will continue to burn for some time!

Tornado, a relative youngster at three years of age, still has pulling power – young, old, parents, enthusiasts or merely 'customers' on a day out, all firing questions at the train crew. Deliberately positioning my wife and dog (both of whom are well used to the scenario) near the sharp end, sound-wise – for one glorious hour I relived the past by leaning (nowadays with goggles) out of the window. All the associated memories came flooding back – the deafening exhaust echoing off of the cuttings and trees, the atmosphere, the heady nectar of grit, smoke and steam emanating from a living machine. It is beyond my comprehension as to how anyone cannot be in awe of the power and presence of a steam locomotive hard at work against the gradient. Visiting locomotives up for gala events will, rather than by chance, work as booked – excepting the occasional unforeseen failure. Perhaps seeming a little ungrateful, what is missing is hope and expectancy associated with a 'surprise' catch – steam rather than diesel or an engine a long way from home. That aside, steam train enthusiasm has nurtured, from a hobby demonised by comedians, into a more acceptable variant of trainspotting with expensive camera and video equipment often being purchased solely for purpose. My current stats (at the time of writing) are 1,224 locomotives for 99,090 miles – how are yours? Happy hunting!

GLOSSARY OF TERMS

Feedback from my first book, purchased by non-railway enthusiasts, revealed that some of the terminology and many of the abbreviations left them more than mystified. This page is for them.

ASLEF	Associated Society of Engineers and Firemen (trade union)	**Mogul**	Locomotive wheel arrangement. Two leading wheels, six powered and coupled driving wheels and no trailing wheels (2–6–0)
ATOC	Association of Train Operating Companies		
BR	British Rail(ways) (1948–97)	**NUR**	National Union of Railwaymen (now part of RMT)
BTC	British Transport Commission	**ORR**	Office of Rail Regulation
4-COR	4-car corridor electric unit (built for the Portsmouth electrification of 1937)	**P**	Power ratio for passenger traffic
		Pacific	Locomotive wheel arrangement. Four leading wheels, six powered and coupled driving wheels and two trailing wheels (4–6–2)
DEMU	Diesel Electric Multiple Unit		
DMO	Divisional Manager's Office		
DMU	Diesel (mechanical) Multiple Unit	**PT**	Pannier tank
ECML	East Coast Main Line (King's Cross to Edinburgh via York)	**RCTS**	The Railway Correspondence and Travel Society
EDL	Electric Diesel Locomotive	**S&D**	Somerset & Dorset Joint Railway (1875–1923)
EMU	Electric multiple unit	**SCTS**	Southern Counties Touring Society
ECS	Empty coaching stock	**SE&CR**	South Eastern & Chatham Railway (1899–1923)
EWD	Each weekday (Mondays to Saturdays)		
F	Power ratio for freight traffic	**SLW**	Single line working
GWR	Great Western Railway (1923–47)	**SR**	Southern Railway (1923–47) or Southern Region of BR (1948–92)
IOWSR	Isle of Wight Steam Railway		
LB&SCR	London, Brighton & South Coast Railway (1846–1922)	**ST**	Saddle tank
		Sustrans	National cycle network
LCGB	The Locomotive Club of Great Britain	**SX**	Saturdays excepted (Mondays to Fridays)
LMR	London Midland Region of BR (1923–47)	**T**	Tank
		TC	Trailer corridor (non-powered)
LMS	London Midland & Scottish Railway (1923–47)	**TOPS**	Total operations processing system
		WCML	West Coast Main Line (Euston to Glasgow via Crewe)
LNER	London & North Eastern Railway (1923–47)		
		WD	War Department
LT&S	London, Tilbury & Southend Railway (1854–1923)	**WR**	Western Region of BR (1948–92)
		WTT	Working timetable (as compared with public)
MT	Mixed traffic (passenger and freight)	**YHA**	Youth Hostels Association

APPENDICES

Appendix I

Maps of the Southern Region

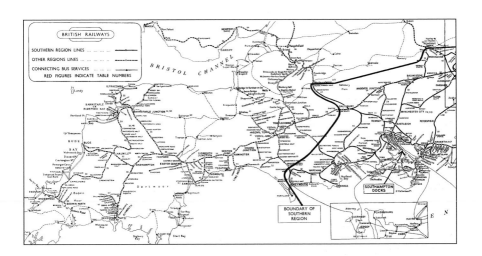

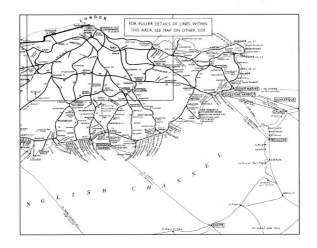

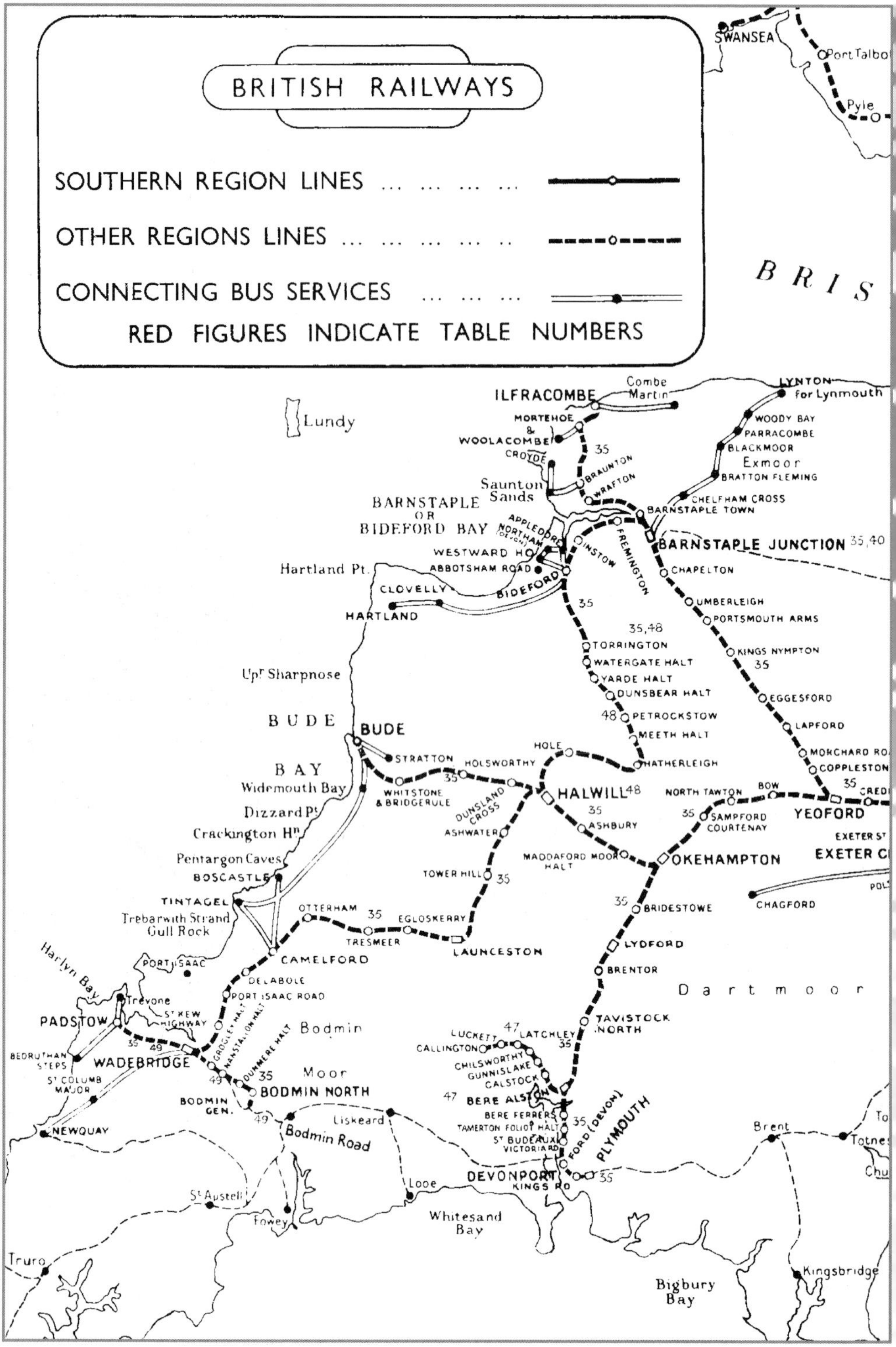
BRITISH RAILWAYS
SOUTHERN REGION LINES
OTHER REGIONS LINES
CONNECTING BUS SERVICES
RED FIGURES INDICATE TABLE NUMBERS
SWANSEA
Port Talbot
Pyle
BRIS
Lundy
ILFRACOMBE
Combe Martin
LYNTON for Lynmouth
MORTEHOE & WOOLACOMBE
CROYDE
BRAUNTON
WRAFTON
Saunton Sands
BARNSTAPLE OR BIDEFORD BAY
APPLEDORE
NORTHAM (DEVON)
WESTWARD HO
ABBOTSHAM ROAD
INSTOW
FREMINGTON
BARNSTAPLE TOWN
BARNSTAPLE JUNCTION 35,40
WOODY BAY
PARRACOMBE
BLACKMOOR
Exmoor
BRATTON FLEMING
CHELFHAM CROSS
Hartland Pt.
CLOVELLY
BIDEFORD
HARTLAND
CHAPELTON
UMBERLEIGH
PORTSMOUTH ARMS
KINGS NYMPTON
EGGESFORD
LAPFORD
MORCHARD ROAD
COPPLESTONE
TORRINGTON
WATERGATE HALT
YARDE HALT
DUNSBEAR HALT
PETROCKSTOW
MEETH HALT
HATHERLEIGH
HOLE
Upr Sharpnose
BUDE
BUDE BAY
Widemouth Bay
Dizzard Pt
Crackington Hn
Pentargon Caves
BOSCASTLE
TINTAGEL
Trebarwith Strand
Gull Rock
STRATTON
HOLSWORTHY
WHITSTONE & BRIDGERULE
DUNSLAND CROSS
ASHWATER
TOWER HILL
HALWILL 48
ASHBURY
MADDAFORD MOOR HALT
NORTH TAWTON
BOW
SAMPFORD COURTENAY
YEOFORD
CREDITON
EXETER ST
EXETER C
OKEHAMPTON
CHAGFORD
BRIDESTOWE
LYDFORD
BRENTOR
Dartmoor
TAVISTOCK NORTH
OTTERHAM
EGLOSKERRY
TRESMEER
LAUNCESTON
CAMELFORD
DELABOLE
PORT ISAAC ROAD
PORT ISAAC
Harlyn Bay
Trevone
PADSTOW
ST KEW HIGHWAY
GROGLEY HALT
NANSTALLON HALT
DUNMERE HALT
Bodmin Moor
WADEBRIDGE
BEDRUTHAN STEPS
ST COLUMB MAJOR
NEWQUAY
BODMIN GEN.
BODMIN NORTH
Liskeard
Bodmin Road
St Austell
Fowey
Looe
Truro
LUCKETT
LATCHLEY
CALLINGTON
CHILSWORTHY
GUNNISLAKE
CALSTOCK
BERE ALSTON
BERE FERRERS
TAMERTON FOLIOT HALT
ST BUDEAUX VICTORIA RD
FORD (DEVON)
PLYMOUTH
DEVONPORT KINGS RD
Whitesand Bay
Brent
Totnes
Kingsbridge
Bigbury Bay

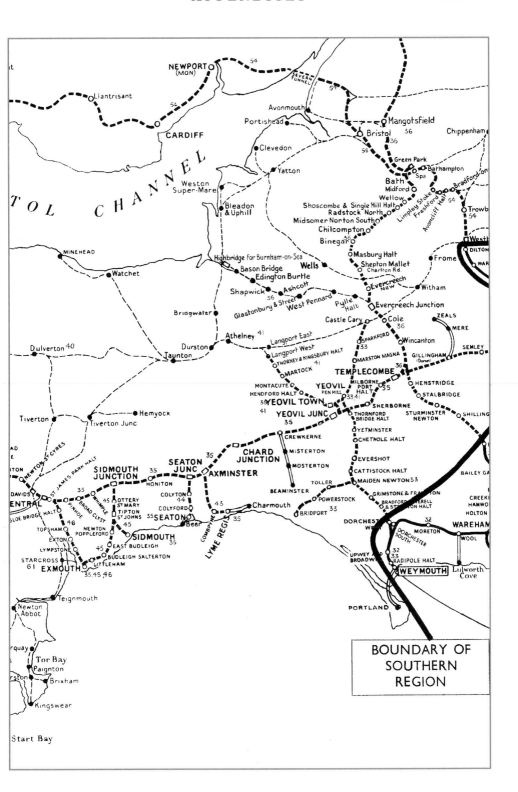

BOUNDARY OF
SOUTHERN
REGION

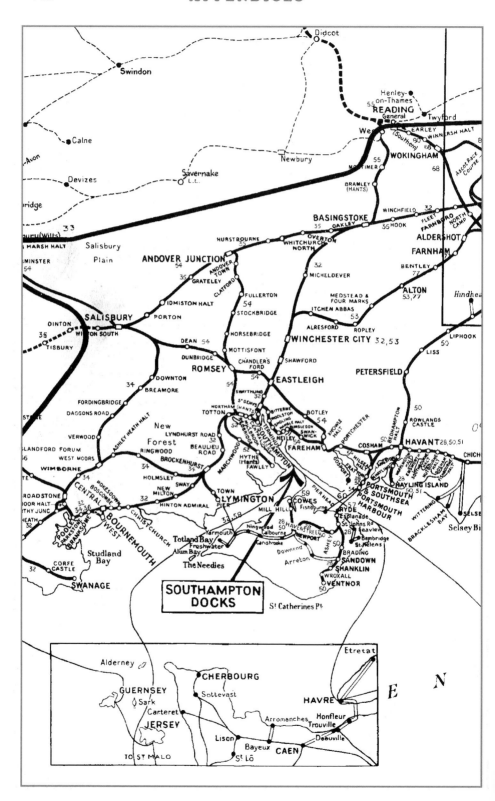

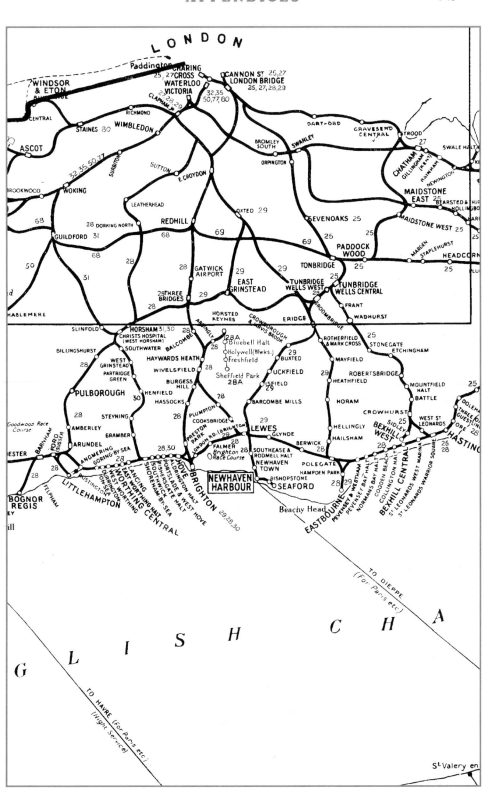

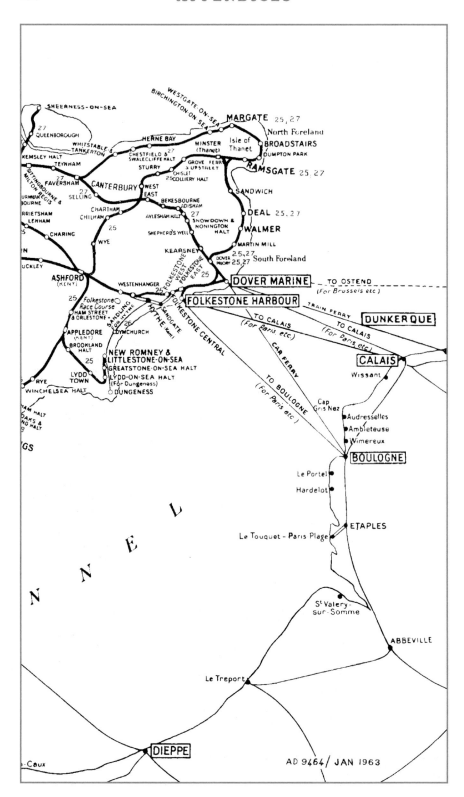

AD 9464/ JAN 1963

Appendix II

Steam locomotives caught on ex-Southern Railway metals on passenger services

Class	Total	Number/Name
2251	1	2218
57xx	1	4694
64xx	1	6412
43xx	1	7306
78xx	2	7813 *Freshford Manor*, 7829 *Ramsbury Manor*
M7	2	30052, 30107
USA	2	30064, 30069
N	11	31405, 31411, 31811, 31816, 31831, 31855, 31858, 31862, 31869, 31873, 31875
U	7	31627, 31639, 31790, 31791, 31792, 31799, 31800
A1X	1	32650
Q1	2	33006, 33020
West Country	41	34001 *Exeter*, 34002 *Salisbury*, 34004 *Yeovil*, 34005 *Barnstaple*, 34006 *Bude*, 34008 *Padstow*, 34009 *Lyme Regis*, 34012 *Launceston*, 34013 *Okehampton*, 34015 *Exmouth*, 34017 *Ilfracombe*, 34018 *Axminster*, 34019 *Bideford*, 34020 *Seaton*, 34021 *Dartmoor*, 34023 *Blackmore Vale*, 34024 *Tamar Valley*, 34025 *Whimple*, 34026 *Yes Tor*, 34032 *Camelford*, 34034 *Honiton*, 34036 *Westward Ho*, 34037 *Clovelly*, 34038 *Lynton*, 34039 *Boscastle*, 34040 *Crewkerne*, 34044 *Woolacombe*, 34046 *Braunton*, 34047 *Callington*, 34048 *Crediton*, 34093 *Saunton*, 34095 *Brentnor*, 34096 *Trevone*, 34097 *Holsworthy*, 34098 *Templecombe*, 34100 *Appledore*, 34101 *Hartland*, 34102 *Lapford*, 34103 *Calstock*, 34104 *Bere Alston*, 34108 *Wincanton*
Battle of Britain	23	34050 *Royal Observer Corps*, 34051 *Winston Churchill*, 34052 *Lord Dowding*, 34053 *Sir Keith Park*, 34054 *Lord Beaverbrook*, 34056 *Croydon*, 34057 *Biggin Hill*, 34059 *Sir Archibald Sinclair*, 34060 *25 Squadron*, 34064 *Fighter Command*, 34066 *Spitfire*, 34070 *Manston*, 34071 *601 Squadron*, 34076 *41 Squadron*, 34077 *603 Squadron*, 34079 *141 Squadron*, 34082 *615 Squadron*, 34084 *253 Squadron*, 34086 *219 Squadron*, 34087 *145 Squadron*, 34088 *213 Squadron*, 34089 *602 Squardon*, 34090 *Sir Eustace Missenden SR*
Merchant Navy	18	35003 *Royal Mail*, 35007 *Aberdeen Commonwealth*, 35008 *Orient Line*, 35010 *Blue Star*, 35011 *General Steam Navigation*, 35012 *United States Line*, 35013 *Blue Funnel*, 35014 *Nederland Line*, 35016 *Elders Fyffes*, 35017 *Belgian Marine*, 35019 *French Line CGT*, 35022 *Holland-America Line*, 35023 *Holland-Afrika Line*, 35026 *Lamport & Holt Line*, 35027 *Port Line*, 35028 *Clan Line*, 35029 *Ellerman Lines*, 35030 *Elder Dempster Lines*
O2	10	W14 *Fishbourne*, W17 *Seaview*, W20 *Shanklin*, W21 *Sandown*, W24 *Calbourne*, W26 *Whitwell*, W27 *Merstone*, W28 *Ashey*, W29 *Alverstone*, W33 *Bembridge*
LMS/2MT	15	41223, 41224, 41230, 41249, 41284, 41287, 41290, 41294, 41295, 41298, 41299, 41312, 41316, 41319, 41320
LMS/4F	1	44422
LMS/5MT	7	44710, 44780, 44872, 44942, 45263, 45299, 45493
LNER A4	1	60024 *Kingfisher*

Class	Total	Number/Name
LNER A2	1	60532 *Blue Peter*
BR/7P6F	1	70004 *William Shakespeare*
BR/5MT	38	73002, 73016, 73018, 73020, 73022, 73028, 73029, 73037, 73043, 73051, 73065, 73068, 73080 *Merlin*, 73081 *Excalibur*, 73082 *Camelot*, 73083 *Pendragon*, 73085 *Melisande*, 73086 *The Green Knight*, 73087 *Linette*, 73088 *Joyous Gard*, 73089 *Maid of Astolat*, 73092, 73093, 73110 *The Red Knight*, 73111 *King Uther*, 73112 *Morgan Le Fay*, 73113 *Lyonesse*, 73114 *Etarre*, 73115 *King Pellinore*, 73117 *Vivien*, 73118 *King Leodegrance*, 73119 *Elaine*, 73133, 73155, 73168, 73169, 73170, 73171,
BR/4MT	10	75068, 75069, 75070, 75072, 75074, 75075, 75076, 75077, 75078, 75079
BR/4MT	25	76005, 76006, 76007, 76008, 76009, 76011, 76013, 76014, 76016, 76018, 76025, 76026, 76030, 76031, 76033, 76053, 76055, 76058, 76060, 76061, 76064, 76065, 76066, 76067, 76069
BR/3MT	1	77014
BR/4MT	30	80011, 80012, 80015, 80016, 80018, 80019, 80032, 80033, 80034, 80041, 80068, 80083, 80085, 80088, 80089, 80094, 80133, 80134, 81038, 80139, 80140, 80141, 80143, 80144, 80145, 80146, 80149, 80151, 80152, 80154
BR/3MT	7	82013, 82019, 82023, 82029, 82041, 82042, 82044
WD	1	600 *Gordon*

No of locos caught = 261: No of journeys made = 1,325: Mileage = 52,770

Appendix III

Traction changes – the final year (July 1966 – July 1967)

I did attempt, having acquired the final Nine Elms running foremen's log, to list all the locomotives working out of Waterloo during Britain's final steam rush hour over the above period. The log, however, for whatever reason was not a comprehensive document and even by filling in the gaps from both personal and friends' observations, resulted in a far from complete list. I can therefore only offer this summary of each train's booked traction during the final year.

Date	17.09	17.23	17.30	17.41	18.00	18.09	18.22	18.30	18.54	19.99
	SX	FO	SX	SX	SX	SX	FO	SX	SX	SX
	Basing	Bomo	Wey	Salis	Salis	Basing	Bomo	Wey	Basing	Exeter
1/7/1966	70D WC	70D WC	70G MN	70E WC	70E WC	70C S5	70D WC	70G MN	70E WC	Class 42
5/9/1966	70A S5		70F MN							
3/10/1966	70G MN	70A S5	Class 47		Class 33+TC	70A WC			Class 33+TC	
14/11/1966			70F WC							
28/11/1966				Class 42 *						70E WC **

Date	17.09 SX Basing	17.23 FO Bomo	17.30 SX Wey	17.41 SX Salis	18.00 SX Salis	18.09 SX Basing	18.22 FO Bomo	18.30 SX Wey	18.54 SX Basing	19.99 SX Exeter
5/12/1966						Class 33 + TC			70A WC	
12/12/1966			Class 47							
2/1/1967	70E WC	70A WC		EMU ***						Class 42
6/3/1967									70G MN	
27/3/1967			EMU +TC							
3/4/1967								Class 47		
1/5/1967									70A WC	
8/5/1967								EMU + TC		
12/6/1967	Class 33						70A WC			

* – worked 19.00 Waterloo/Exeter forward from Salisbury
** – worked to Salisbury only
*** – terminated at Basingstoke
Class 33 – Crompton (D65xx); Class 42 – 'Warship' (D8xx): Class 47 – Brush 4 (D15xx); WC –
'West Country' (including 'Battle of Britain'); MN – 'Merchant Navy'; S5 – BR Standard 5MT
70A – Nine Elms; 70C – Guildford; 70D – Eastleigh; 70E – Salisbury; 70F – Bournemouth; 70G –
Weymouth
Basing – Basingstoke; Bomo – Bournemouth; Wey – Weymouth; Salis – Salisbury

Appendix IV

This Train (No Longer) Terminates Here
A summary of closed lines (to passengers) visited during my travels:

Train service	Closure	Visited	Traction	Notes
Kemp Town	Jan 1933	Jun 1971	DEMU	Rail tour
Shepherdswell/Tilmanstone	Oct 1948	Mar 1968	DL	Rail tour
Gravesend West/Farningham Rd	Aug 1953	Mar 1968	DL	Rail tour
Tenterden/Bodiam	Jan 1954	Often	Steam	Preserved line
Bentley/Bordon	Sep 1957	Apr 1966	Steam	Rail tour
Sheffield Park/Kingscote (z)	Mar 1958	Often	Steam	Preserved line
Andover Jct/Ludgershall	Sep 1961	Mar 1986	Steam	Rail Tour
Hoo Jct/Grain	Dec 1961	Mar 1968	DL	Rail Tour
Horstead Keynes/Haywards Heath	Oct 1963	Sep 1963	EMU	
Havant/Hayling Island	Nov 1963	Oct 1963	Steam	
Brockenhurst/Poole (via Ringwood)	May 1964	Apr 1964	Steam	
Salisbury/West Moors	May 1964	Apr 1964	Steam	
Bexhill West/Crowhurst	Jun 1964	May 1964	DEMU	
Taunton/Yeovil Town	Jun 1964	Apr 1964	Steam	
Torrington/Halwill Jct	Mar 1965	Jul 1964	Steam	
Hailsham/Eridge	Jun 1965	May 1965	Steam	
Guildford/Christ's Hospital	Jun 1965	May 1965	Steam	
Bournemouth West	Oct 1965	Jul 1965	Steam	
Torrington/Barnstaple Jct	Oct 1965	Jul 1964	Steam	
Axminster/Lyme Regis	Nov 1965	Jul 1964	DMU	
Totton/Fawley	Feb 1966	Feb 1966	DEMU	Last train
Cowes/Ryde St Johns Road	Feb 1966	Often	Steam	Part preserved line
Seaton/Seaton Jct	Mar 1966	Jul 1964	DMU	
Bath Green Park/Poole	Mar 1966	Feb 1966	Steam	
Shoreham-by-Sea/Christ's Hospital	Mar 1966	Mar 1966	DEMU	Last day of service
Highbridge/Evercreech Jct	Mar 1966	Sep 1965	Steam	
Ventnor/Shanklin	Apr 1966	Sep 1965	Steam	
Southampton Terminus	Sep 1966	Mar 1966	Steam	
Yeovil Pen Mill/Town/Junction	Oct 1966	Apr 1964	Steam	
Okehampton/Wadebridge	Oct 1966	Jul 1964	Steam	
Halwill Jct/Bude	Oct 1966	Jul 1964	Steam	
Taunton/Barnstaple Jct	Oct 1966	Often	Steam	Part preserved line
Padstow/Bodmin Road	Jan 1967	Jul 1964	DL	Part preserved line
Three Bridges/Groombridge	Jan 1967	Jan 1967	Steam	

Train service	Closure	Visited	Traction	Notes
New Romney/Appledore	Mar 1967	Nov 1963	DEMU	
Exmouth/Sidmouth Jct	Mar 1967	Jul 1964	Steam	
Hailsham/Polegate	Sep 1968	May 1965	Steam	
Uckfield/Lewes	May 1969	Aug 1963	DL	
Eastleigh/Romsey	May 1969	May 1965	DEMU	Reopened Oct 2003
Longmoor Military Railway	Oct 1969	Apr 1966	Steam	
Ilfracombe/Barnstaple Jct	Oct 1970	Jul 1964	DL	
Swanage/Wareham	Jan 1972	Often	Steam	Part preserved line
Okehampton/Yeoford	Jun 1972	Jul 1964	Steam	
Alton/Winchester	Feb 1973	Often	Steam	Part preserved line
Bridport/Maiden Newton	May 1975	Jan 1967	Steam	
Selhurst/Norwood Junction	May 1982	May 1982	EMU	Last train
Woodside/Selsdon	May 1983	May 1983	EMU	Last day of service
Coulsdon North	Sep 1983	Sep 1983	EMU	Last day of service
Tunbridge Wells Central/Eridge	Jul 1985	Often	Steam	Part preserved line
Holborn Viaduct	Jan 1990	Jan 1990	EMU	Last train
Dover Western Docks	Sep 1994	Sep 1994	EMU	
Addiscombe/Elmers End	May 1997	May 1997	EMU	To Tramlink
Wimbledon/West Croydon	May 1997	Often	EMU	To Tramlink
Folkestone Harbour	Mar 2009	Sep 1991	Steam	
Weymouth Quay	2010	Sep 1967	DL	

(z) = Extended to East Grinstead during 2013
1964 saw the greatest BR milage loss (1,058) followed by 1962 (780) and 1966 (750)
Source: *Beeching: 50 Years of the Axeman* by Robin Jones, Morton Books.

The 15 October 1964 General Election saw Harold Wilson of Labour take control of the country with a majority of four seats. The newly-elected government had promised in their manifesto to halt the closures proposed by the Conservative-appointed Dr Beeching. The hopes, however, of the affected communities for a reprieve were short-lived. Transport Minister Barbara Castle failed to stop the flood of closures.

Appendix V

Motive power depot visits

I was never a 'spotter' in respect of number taking, i.e. standing on platform ends or at linesides 'copping' all passing train numbers, be they steam, diesel or electric, and red-lining the entries in one of Ian Allan's ABCs. Hordes of enthusiasts used to go on organised coach trips specifically aimed at 'bashing' the depots and proudly exhibited their books with the results to anyone fool enough to ask to see them. My six shed visits (with the exception of Feltham where it was the only establishment to view to doomed S15 class) were undertaken because sufficient time within my schedule was available. With instructions as how to get there extracted from the *British Locomotive Shed Directory* (1965, thirteenth edition as published by Ian Allan) they were, in date order, as follows:

Depot	Date/time
Templecombe (83G)	Sat 17 July 1965 – 05.00 hours
In steam	41283/90/1/307, 47806, 75072, 80037/41/3/59
Dead	41216
Stored	9647/70, 41208/14/43, 80067
Diesels	Nil

The shed is on the east side of the Wincanton–Henstridge line north of the point where it goes under the main Waterloo–Exeter line. The yard is visible from the Wincanton–Henstridge line and the connecting spur. Turn left outside the main line station along the approach road. Turn left under the railway bridge and the first right before the second railway over-bridge. A broad path leads to the shed from the left-hand side of this road. Walking time 5 minutes.

Depot	Date/time
Feltham (70B)	Fri 13 Aug 1965 – 10.00 hours
In steam	30838/9, 75077
Dead	30837, 34012 *Launceston*, 34100 *Appledore*, 76011, 80011/9/33/4/89/140/1
Stored	30833, 76030
Diesels	D3273, D6536/56

The shed is on the south side of the line east of the station. The yard is partially visible from the line. Go straight ahead outside Hounslow station along Station Road and turn left into Hanworth Road. Continue along this road for about a mile, and a drive leads to the shed from the right-hand side, opposite the junction of Powder Mill Road. Walking time 25 minutes. The nos 110 and 111 bus routes operate along Hanworth Lane.

Depot	Date/time
Bath Green Park (82F)	Sat 18 Sep 1965 – 09.00 hours
In steam	3659/758, 48309/444, 73001/68, 80059, 82041
Dead	47506, 48706/32/760, 82004
Stored	73015/51/4
Diesels	Nil

The shed is on the north side of the line west of Bath Green Park station. The yard is visible from the line. Turn right outside the station along Midland Bridge Road. Turn right into Lower Bristol Road and right again into Bridge Road. A cinder path leads to the shed from the right-hand side of this road just past the railway bridge. Walking time 10 minutes.

Depot	Date/time
Salisbury (70E)	Sun 4 April 1966 – 15.00 hours
On shed	31411, 31639, 33006, 34006 *Bude*, 34026 *Yes Tor*, 34056 *Croydon*, 34066 *Spitfire*, 34089 *602 Squadron*, 34100 *Appledore*, 34108 *Wincanton*, 73065/169, 76007/8/12/8/59/67, 80152
Stored	34076 *41 Squadron*, 75066
Diesels	D807 *Caradoc*, D1922, D2179, D6505/24/33, 15230/1

The shed is on the south side of the line west of the station. The yard is visible from the line. Cross the station yard, descend a flight of steps into Churchfields Road, and turn right. Continue parallel to the railway and the shed entrance is on the right-hand side at the corner of Cherry Orchard Lane. Walking time 10 minutes.

Depot	Date/time
Bournemouth (70F)	Sat 10 Dec 1966 – 14.00 hours
In steam	34098 *Templecombe*, 34104 *Bere Alston*, 35023 *Holland-Afrika Line*, 41224/30/95/320, 73155, 76005/11, 80032
Dead	34024 *Tamar Valley*, 34040 *Crewkerne*, 76026, 80011/146

The shed is on the north side of the line at Bournemouth Central station. The yard is visible from the line. The shed entrance is a gate at the end of the yard on the northern (Up) side of Bournemouth Central station. Walking time less than 5 minutes.

Depot	Date/time
Bournemouth (70F)	Saturday 14 Jan 1967 – 14.45 hours
In steam	34001 *Exeter*, 34019 *Bideford*, 34044 *Woolacombe*, 34108 *Wincanton*, 41224/312, 73002, 76053/66, 80011
Dead	34024 *Tamar Valley*, 41230/95/320, 76011/26, 80032/134

All gone – car parks, industrial estates, supermarkets, etc.

Appendix VI

The Author's Service History

(Southern Region unless indicated)

Date	Location	Duties
06/62	Fares Section, DMO (SWD), Waterloo	Publicity bills, excursion and fare enquires and general errand boy
01/63	Travel Facilities, DMO (SWD), Waterloo	Travel enquiries, camping coaches, CTEB relief clerk
02/66	Standard Timings, DMO (SED), Queen Street	Journal marker, performance statistics and analysis
11/66	Special Traffic, DMO (SWD), Wimbledon	Notice production, special train timings
10/67	Diagrams, DMO (SWD), Wimbledon	Engine and crew diagramming
02/68	Freight Section, DMO (SWD), Wimbledon	Displaced into travelling wagon auditing position
04/68	Central Crew Rosters, GMO Waterloo	Diagramming for South Eastern Division services
09/73	Performance Section, GMO Crewe (LMR)	Performance issues, Inspection and Royal train arrangements
06/77	Industrial Relations, GMO Euston (LMR)	Agenda compilation for union reps, mileage claims, loss of earnings, Sunday rotations, etc.
10/78	Performance Section, DMO Euston (LMR)	Emergency train plans, VIP/Royal train arrangements, Inspection Specials
09/80	Central Crew Rosters, GMO Waterloo	Diagramming for South Eastern Division services
12/82	Central Crew Rosters, GMO Waterloo	Diagramming manager for all non-EMU services on SE & CTL services
02/93	NSE, Friars Bridge Court, Blackfriars	Displaced into Engineering Trains Planning Manager position
04/94	Railfreight Distribution, Paddington (RfD)	National diagramming for automotive, intermodal and Channel Tunnel services
10/96	Train Planning, Croydon NSE/Connex/Southern	Special Traffic diagramming for ex-Central Division services
06/07	Retirement	Article/book writing

DMO – Divisional Managers Office; SWD – South Western Division; SED – South Eastern Division; GMO – General Managers Office; NSE – Network South East; LMR – London Midland Region; RfD – Railfreight Distribution; EMU – electric multiple units; CTEB – Central Telephone Enquiry Bureau; SE – South Eastern; CTL – Central division.

SOURCES

Engine Shed Society

British Railways Steam Locomotives 1948–1968 by Hugh Longworth;
Southern Steam Surrender by John H. Bird

To view my pre-1968 BR steam scenes please visit www.southern-images.co.uk –
then type WIDDOWSON in the search box. To view all my photographs please visit
http:mistermixedtraction.smugmug.com, then select one of the twenty galleries
including the West County, Scotland and France. Simply click on 'slideshow', sit
back and enjoy.

ABOUT THE AUTHOR

Keith Widdowson was born, to his pharmacist father and secretarial mother, during the calamitous winter of 1947 at St Mary Cray, Kent – attending the nearby schools of Poverest and Charterhouse. He joined British Railways in June 1962 as an enquiry clerk at the Waterloo telephone bureau – 'because his mother had noted his obsession with collecting timetables'.

Thus began a forty-five-year career within various train planning departments throughout BR, the bulk of which was at Waterloo but also included locations at Cannon Street, Wimbledon, Crewe, Euston, Blackfriars, Paddington and finally Croydon – specialising in dealing with train crew arrangements. After spending several years during the 1970s and '80s in Cheshire, London and Sittingbourne he returned to his roots in 1985 where he finally met the steadying influence in his life, Joan, with whom he had a daughter, Victoria. In addition to membership of the local residents' association (St Pauls Cray), the Sittingbourne & Kemsley Light Railway and the U3A organisation, he keeps busy writing articles for railway magazines and gardening.